The Rock House Method

Presents

Learn Bass 1
The Method for a New Generation

1

Written & Method By:
John McCarthy

Adapted By: Jimmy Rutkowski
Supervising Editor: Joe Palombo
Music Transcribing & Engraving: Jimmy Rutkowski
Production Manager: Joe Palombo
Layout, Graphics & Design: Jimmy Rutkowski
Photography: Jimmy Rutkowski, Rodney Dabney
Copy Editors: Cathy McCarthy

Cover Art Direction & Design:
Jimmy Rutkowski

HL00102681
ISBN: 978-1-4768-1427-8
Produced by The Rock House Method®

Table of Contents

Words from the Author

Playing music is a rewarding art form that will last you a lifetime, I discovered that fact shortly after I was given my first instrument. I have spent my career sharing the passion I have for music with others. With my teaching method, I truly believe you too will enjoy years of fun and will pass on the passion you discover. If you follow the method step-by step you will be successful and enjoy playing bass for years to come. When I designed The Rock House Method, my mission was to create the most complete and fun way to learn. I accomplished this by developing and systematically arranging a modern method based on the needs and social demands of today's players. I not only tell you where to put your fingers, I show you ways to use what you learn so that you can make music right from the start. I know it is hard to imagine, but even the all-time greats started somewhere, there was a time when they too didn't even know what a chord was. As you progress as a bass player, keep your mind open to all styles of music. Set-up a practice schedule that you can manage, be consistent, challenge yourself and realize everyone learns at a different rate. Be patient, persistent and remember music is supposed to be fun!

NOW, GET EXCITED, this is it. YOU are going to play bass!

John McCarthy

Digital eBook

When you register this product at the lesson support site RockHouseSchool.com, you will receive a digital version of this book. This interactive eBook can be used on all devices that support Adobe PDF. This will allow you to access your book using the latest portable technology any time you want.

The Rock House Method Learning System

This learning system can be used on your own or guided by a teacher. Be sure to register for your free lesson support at RockHouseSchool.com. Your member number can be found inside the cover of this book.

Lesson Support Site: Once registered, you can use this fully interactive site along with your product to enhance your learning experience, expand your knowledge, link with instructors, and connect with a community of people around the world who are learning to play music using The Rock House Method®.

Quick Start Video: The quick start video is designed to guide you through your first steps! All the basic information you will need to get playing now is demonstrated.

Gear Education Video: Walking into a music store can be an intimidating endeavor for someone starting out. To help you, Rock House has a series of videos to educate you on some of the gear you will encounter as you start your musical journey.

Bass Care Video: This video will help you with the care and maintenance of your instrument. From changing strings to cleaning your bass, you'll learn many helpful tips.

Quizzes: Each level of the curriculum contains multiple quizzes to gauge your progress. When you see a quiz icon go to the *Lesson Support* site and take the quiz. It will be graded and emailed to you for review.

Audio Examples & Play Along Tracks: Demonstrations of how each lesson should sound and full band backing tracks to play certain lessons over. These audio tracks are available on the accompanying mp3 CD.

Icon Key

These tell you there is additional information and learning utilities available at RockHouseSchool.com to support that lesson.

Backing Track

CD Track Backing track icons are placed on lessons where there is an audio demonstration to let you hear what that lesson should sound like or a backing track to play the lesson over. Use these audio tracks to guide you through the lessons. **This is an mp3 CD, it can be played on any computer and all mp3 disc compatible playback devices.**

Metronome

Metronome icons are placed next to the examples that we recommend you practice using a metronome. You can download a free, adjustable metronome on the *Lesson Support* site.

Worksheet

Worksheets are a great tool to help you thoroughly learn and understand music. These worksheets can be downloaded at the *Lesson Support* site.

Tuner

You can download the free online tuner on the *Lesson Support* site to help tune your instrument.

Parts of the Bass

A bass is made up of three main sections: the body, the neck and the headstock. All of the other parts of the bass are mounted on these three sections.

Body   Neck   Head

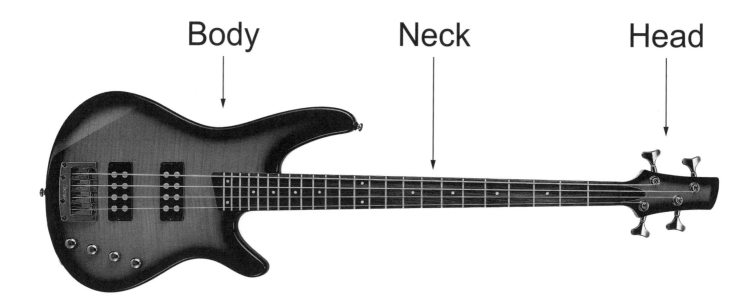

The bridge is the assembly that anchors the strings to the body. Pickups are also mounted to the body and work like little microphones that pick up the sound from the strings. A cable is plugged into the bass's input jack to send the signal into the amp. Most bass guitars will also have a pickup selector switch along with volume and tone knobs. A strap can be attached to the strap buttons to play the bass standing up.

The metal bars that go across the neck are called frets. The dots between certain frets are called position markers and help you know where your hand is on the neck while playing. At the end of the neck is the nut which guides the strings onto the headstock and keeps them in place. On the headstock, the strings are wound around the tuning posts, and the tuners (also called machine heads) are used to tune the strings to pitch.

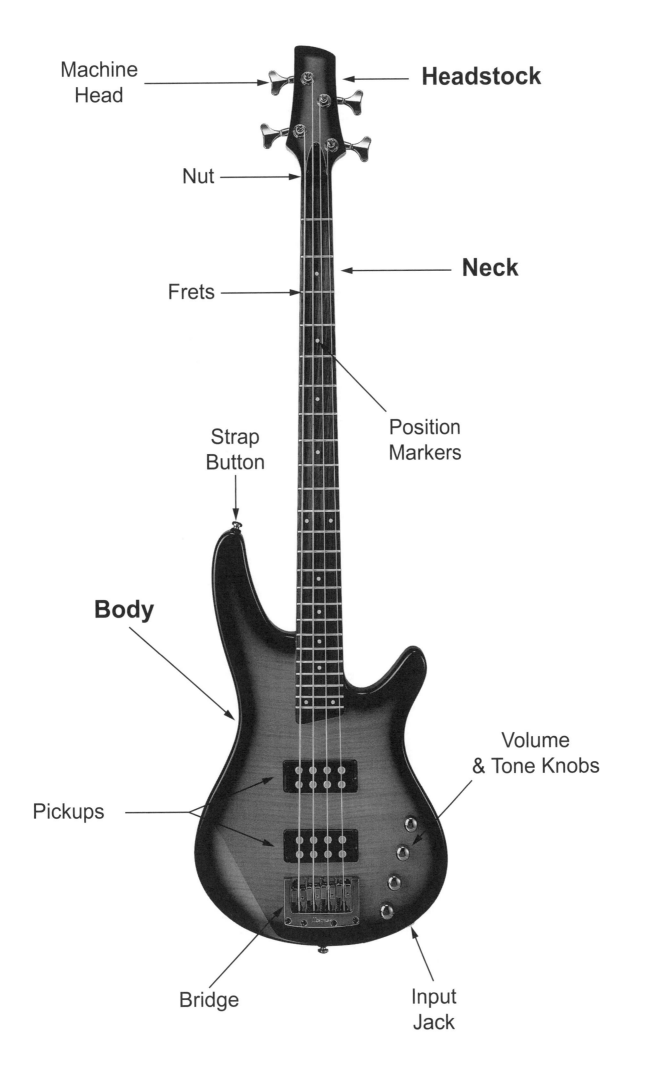

Machine Head

Headstock

Nut

Neck

Frets

Position Markers

Strap Button

Body

Volume & Tone Knobs

Pickups

Bridge

Input Jack

Holding the Bass

Throughout this book, we will refer to the picking hand as your right hand, and the hand fretting the notes as your left hand. When sitting find a comfortable chair with no arms and make sure you can sit with your feet planted flat on the ground. Hold the bass neck up at a 30 degree angle.

Right Hand Position

Drape your arm and hand over the strings almost parallel with the bridge. Keep your thumb planted either on top of the pickup or thumb plate if your bass has one.

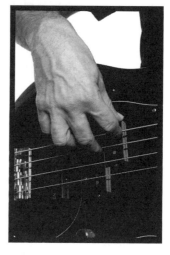

Left Hand Position

Hold your left hand out in front of you with your wrist straight and your fingers curled in to make a "C" shape with your hand.

Place the first joint of your thumb against the back of the neck. Don't bend or contort your wrist; only the tips of your fingers should touch the strings.

Names of the Open Strings & Tuning

The fattest string is the 4th string and the thinnest is the 1st string. A great way to remember the open strings is to use an acronym creating a word for each letter name. The following is an acronym I created: Good – Days – Are – Exciting. Make up you own saying for the open strings.

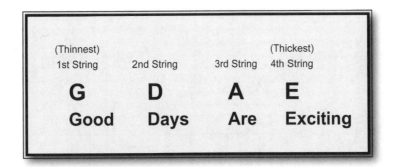

Tune your bass using the machine heads on the headstock. Turn the machine heads a little bit at a time while plucking the string and listening to the change in pitch. Tighten the string to raise the pitch. Loosen the string to lower the pitch. The easiest way to tune a bass is to use an electronic tuner. You can download a free tuner from the *Lesson Support* site RockHouseSchool.com.

Finger Numbers

As you progress through this book I will be referencing your left hand fingers with numbers. It is very important for you to memorize these now so you can follow along with ease. To the right are the numbers that correspond with your fingers.

Fretting hand:

Index finger = 1 Middle finger = 2
Ring finger = 3 Pinky finger = 4

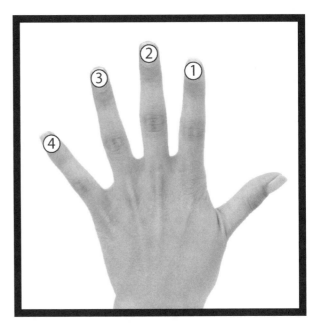

Reading Tablature

Tablature (or tab) is a number system for reading bass sheet music. The four lines of the tablature staff represent each of the strings on the bass. The top line is the thinnest (highest pitched) string. The bottom line is the thickest (lowest pitched) string. The numbers placed directly on these lines are the fret number to play each note. Underneath the staff, is a series of numbers. These numbers tell you which left hand finger to fret the notes with.

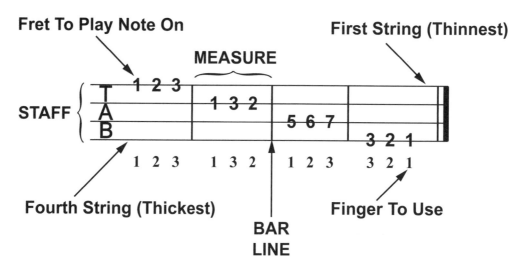

Muting

Muting is a technique that helps you control the strings from unwanted notes and string noise. The basic concept is to lightly touch your hand on the strings that you are not playing. You can do this with your left or right hand. Play the next exercise and as you switch strings mute or deaden the other strings so only the string you are playing is sounded.

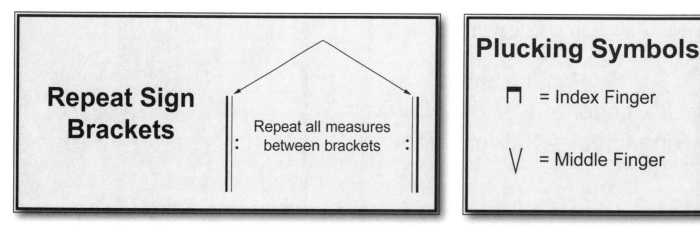

Repeat Sign Brackets

Repeat all measures between brackets

Plucking Symbols

⊓ = Index Finger

∨ = Middle Finger

Alternating

Alternating is picking (plucking) with your index and middle fingers repetitively. You can play notes effectively and with speed by using your fingers in this manner. Play through the exercise below using open strings in four note patterns:

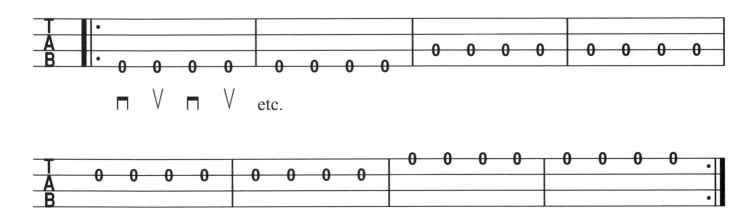

Counting Beats

A beat is the basic unit of time in music. A common way to count beats is to tap your foot. One beat would equal tapping your foot down-up. Tap your foot and count 1 – 2 – 3 – 4 repetitively, say each number as your foot hits the ground. You will learn different note types that tell you how many beats to let notes ring.

Foot Down

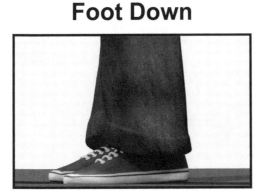

Foot Up

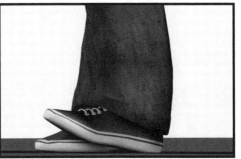

The Metronome

A metronome is a device that clicks at an adjustable rate you set. It will help you develop a sense of timing and gauge your progress. By playing along with the "clicking" sound you get the sense of playing with another musician. Each click represents one beat. I will note the best times to use a metronome throughout this program with a metronome icon. If you don't have a metronome you can download one for **free** from the *Lesson Support* website.

Timing Explanations – Note Values

The Parts of a Note

The HEAD
The STEM
The FLAG

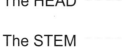

The Types of Notes

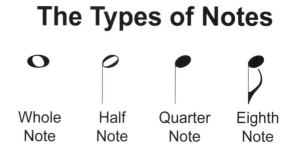

Whole Note   Half Note   Quarter Note   Eighth Note

Whole Notes = 4 Beats

This is a Whole Note. The head is hollow and there is no stem or flag. A Whole Note will receive four beats or counts.

Half Notes = 2 Beats

This is a Half Note. The head is hollow and there is a stem. A Half Note will receive two beats or counts.

Quarter Notes = 1 Beat

This is a Quarter Note. The head is solid and there is a stem. A Quarter Note will receive one beat or count.

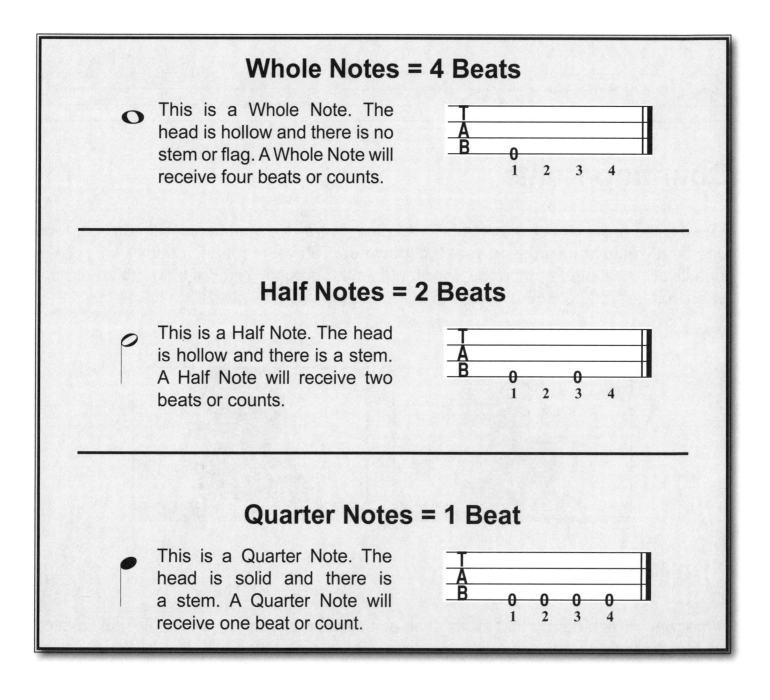

Notation in Tab

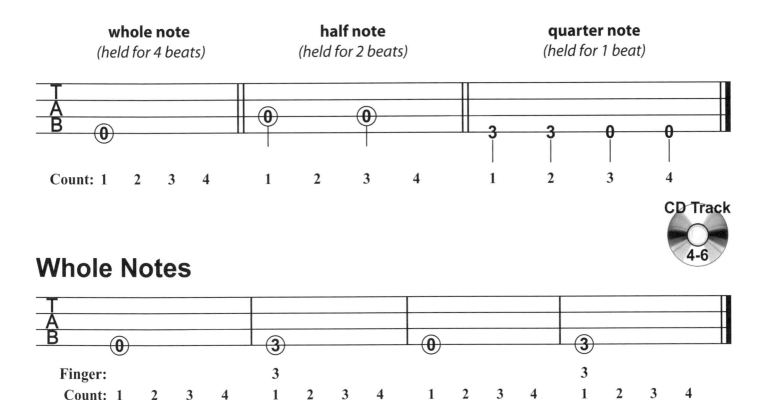

whole note	half note	quarter note
(held for 4 beats)	*(held for 2 beats)*	*(held for 1 beat)*

CD Track
4-6

Whole Notes

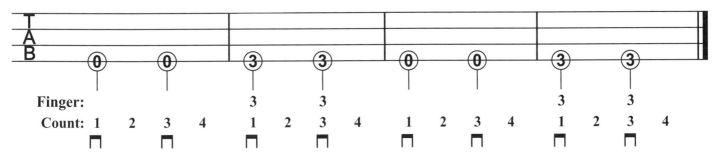

Half Notes

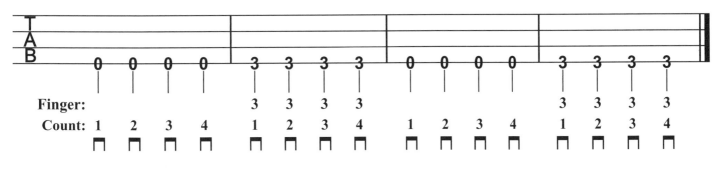

Quarter Notes

Your First Bass Line

Get excited! It's time to learn your first bass line. This bass line is played using alternate plucking in steady quarter notes. Follow the tablature below and be sure to use the proper finger for each note. Once you can play this without hesitation play it along with the backing track to create a full band sound.

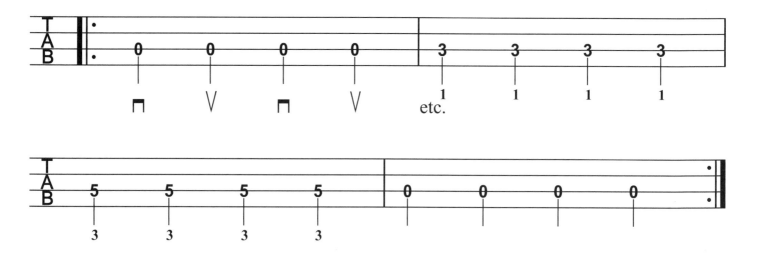

Time Signatures

Time signatures are written at the beginning of a piece of music. The sole function of a time signature is to tell you how to count the music you are about to play. The top number tells you how many beats there are in each measure and the bottom number tells what type of beat is receiving the count.

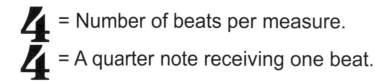

$\dfrac{4}{4}$ = Number of beats per measure.

$\dfrac{4}{4}$ = A quarter note receiving one beat.

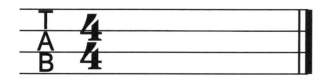

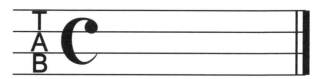

Indicates four beats per measure.

Four beats per measure. Also known as "common time."

Counting with a Drum Beat

Now you will count along with a drum beat. The drum beat used for this lesson is the most common timing 4/4. This means it is divided into four beat sections (or measures). Notice the 4/4 at the beginning of the staff below, this will be on all music that is in this time signature. As the drum beat is playing count 1 – 2 – 3 – 4 and repeat this count. The 1 & 3 are counted when you hear the bass drum which is the big bass toned drum; while 2 & 4 are counted on the snare drum which is the higher pitched drum that has a bit of rattle to its sound.

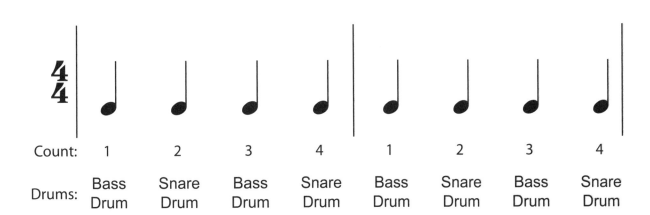

	Count:	1	2	3	4	1	2	3	4
Drums:		Bass Drum	Snare Drum	Bass Drum	Snare Drum	Bass Drum	Snare Drum	Bass Drum	Snare Drum

Body Clock

Now get your "Body Clock" into the mix. Your body clock is basically moving your body to the music. One of the simplest ways to do this is by tapping your foot.

With the same drum backing track count and tap your foot. Every count should be when your foot hits the ground, like you are stepping on it. One beat equals one down-up movement of your foot. Another common way to use your body clock is to bob your head along with the beat.

MUSIC ASSIGNMENT

This is a very common drum beat and is used in most popular music. After you feel comfortable tapping and counting along with the backing track do this same thing with your favorite songs or music you hear on the radio. Take notice to the "drums specifically" within the musical piece; listen for the bass drum and snare drum, these two drums are usually the backbone for a song's rhythm. Try to dissect the music and hear it as many parts coming together to form a song instead of one big sound.

Rhythm – Playing with the Drums

In a drum beat the bass drum and snare drum are the back bone of the beat. You must learn the sound of these drums because you will play along with them to create a solid foundation for songs.

In Example 1 use the drum backing track to play the open 4th string along with the bass drum. The bass drum will hit on beats 1 and 3.

Example 1

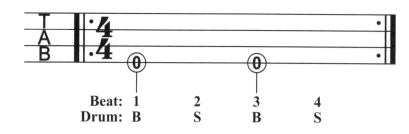

In Example 2 you will play along with the bass and snare drum. The bass drum still hits on beats 1 and 3 while the snare drum hits on beats 2 and 4.

Example 2

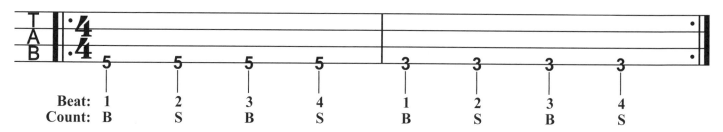

Bass Line #2

Gear Shifter

The following is a quarter note bass line. Make sure to use alternate plucking.

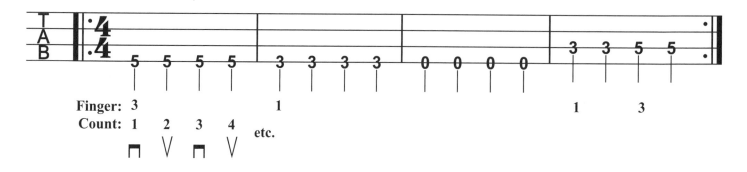

Blues Progression

Blues has influenced almost every genre of music. A basic understanding of the blues will give you a great advantage as a bassist. The following blues progression is played using a series of open strings. This is a 12 bar blues progression which means it consists of 12 measures. This progression should sound familiar; it's the foundation for many rock and blues songs.

First play through the progression with a straight feel, which is an even steady pattern. Make sure to use alternate plucking.

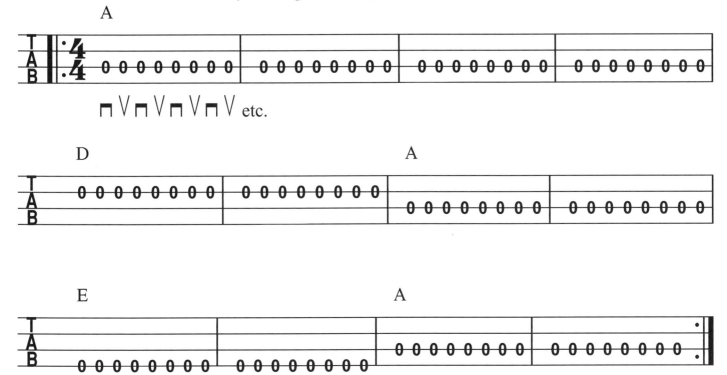

Shuffle Feel

The shuffle feel is an uneven rhythm that creates a sway to a song. This rhythm is found in countless blues and rock songs. Play the measure below using the open 3rd string to get familiar with this rhythm feel, the way the notes are spaced depicts the timing.

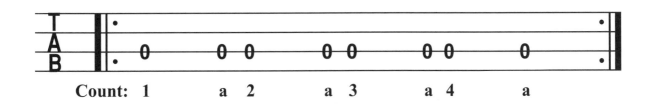

Blues Shuffle Progression

Now apply the shuffle feel to the blues progression. The shuffle feel is also called the swing feel. Pay close attention when going to each new measure, the last note of each measure should flow to the first note of the new measure seemlessly.

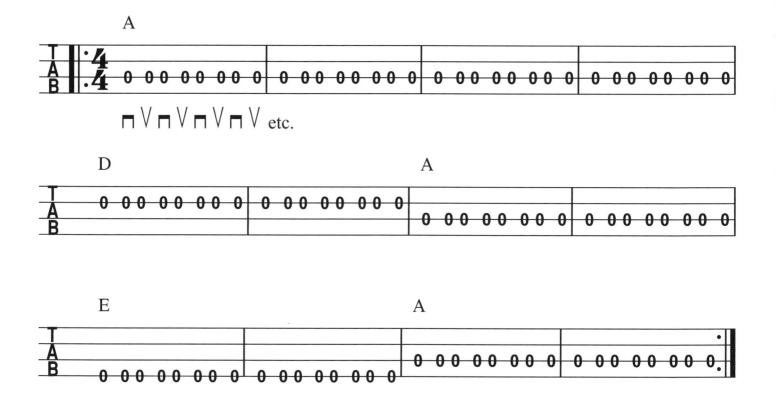

MUSIC ASSIGNMENT

Listen to your favorite music and try to hear the blues influence. There is a blues influence in almost every genre of music. After you play this rhythm with both a straight and shuffle feel you will easily play the blues feel in songs you learn in the future.

Learn Bass 1 - Quiz 1
Once you complete this section go to RockHouseSchool.com and take the quiz to track your progress. You will receive an email with your results and suggestions.

Attaching Your Strap

To stand up and play you must attach a strap to your bass. Most bass guitars have strap buttons on both sides of the body of the bass. Simply attach the strap to each side of the bass at these buttons.

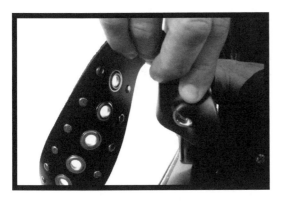

Most straps are adjustable and should be set to a comfortable height. A good starting point is to look at how the bass rests against your body when sitting down and duplicate this position when you stand up. You may think it looks cooler to have the bass positioned lower (like some of your favorite bassists) but at this stage it will make learning more difficult. Remember that you should always have the neck of your bass pointed up at about a 30 degree angle (sitting or standing) to ensure proper hand position.

Finger Flexing

CD Track 21

Here is an exercise that will help develop the strength and coordination of your hands. This exercise is a 5 – 7 – 6 – 7 fret pattern repeated on each string. You should use alternate plucking continuously. There are two plucking patterns below the staff. Make sure to practice both patterns. Take your time and increase your speed in small increments. This would be a great lesson to play along with a metronome.

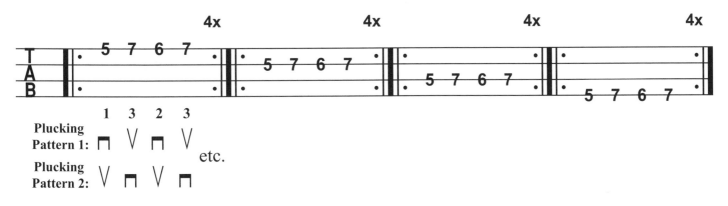

19

MUSIC ASSIGNMENT

Once you can play this pattern smoothly across all four strings move it one fret lower starting on the 4th fret and playing frets 4 – 6 – 5 – 6 down each string. The distance between the frets gets wider as you move toward the nut; this will help stretch your hands reach to play difficult passages in songs. Keep moving it down as you feel comfortable with the fret position until you reach the first fret.

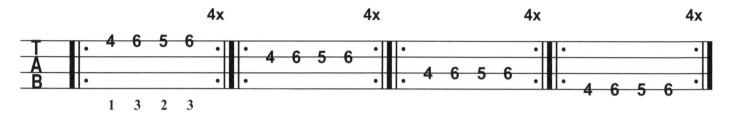

Bass Line #3

CD Track
22-24

Hit it Hard

Here is another bass line to challenge your fingers. Once you can play this steady all the way through play it with the backing track to apply it in a band fashion. Again there are two plucking patterns below the staff. Both patterns are alternate plucking, the difference is that one begins with your index finger and the other with your middle finger.

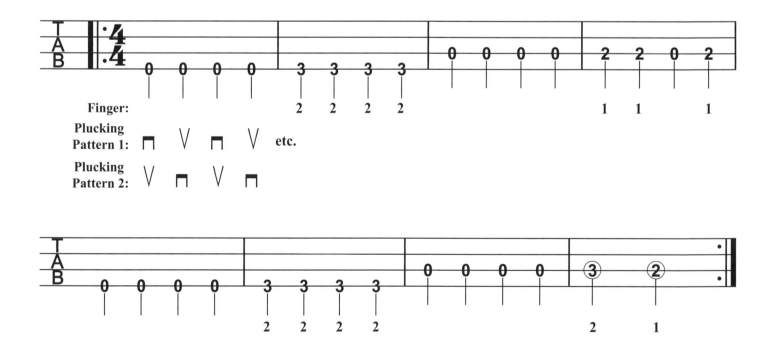

20

Eighth Notes

An eighth note receives ½ beat of sound and divides a quarter note in half. For every one beat you will hit two notes. You will also use a different kind of counting. Instead of one, two, three, four, sub-divide that in half and count one & two & three & four &. The one, two, three and four are when your foot hits the ground, each "&" is when your foot goes up in the air.

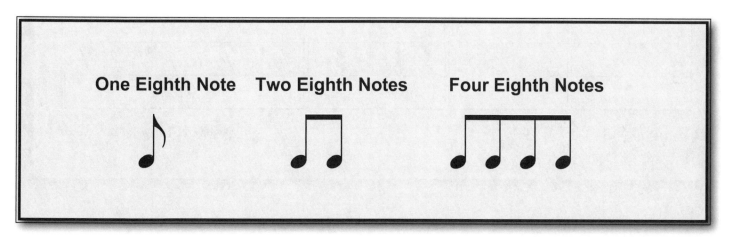

Here is an exercise playing eighth notes. While plucking your 3rd string open tap your foot and play it in eighth notes. Use alternate plucking while you do this to get speed and fluidity.

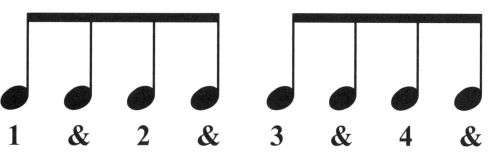

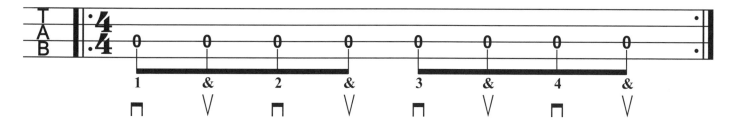

MUSIC ASSIGNMENT

Now that you are playing eighth notes play them along with the drum beat used in the "Counting with a Drum Beat" lesson. While the drum beat is playing, pick eighth notes starting on the low E string and then down all four strings. Make sure to tap your foot along to get your body clock into motion. Use alternate plucking.

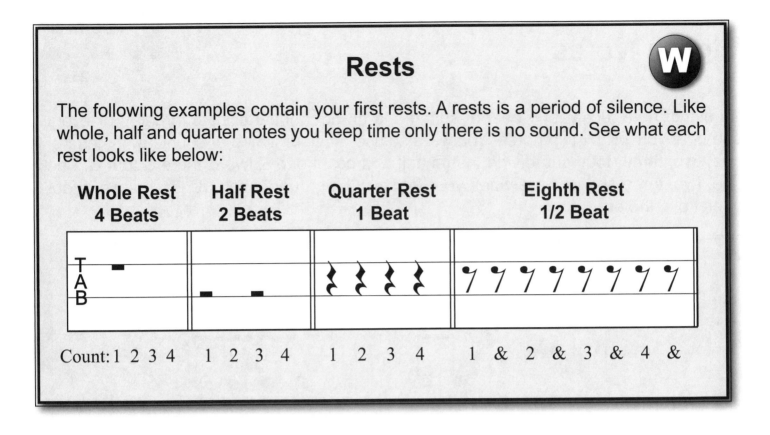

Rests

The following examples contain your first rests. A rests is a period of silence. Like whole, half and quarter notes you keep time only there is no sound. See what each rest looks like below:

Rhythm – Playing Eighth Notes

CD Track 26-27

When playing eighth notes in a bass line you can create syncopated rhythms. These rhythms contain notes played on the up beat or "&" count. In example 1 you will play notes on the 1 – 3 – & counts along with the drum backing track.

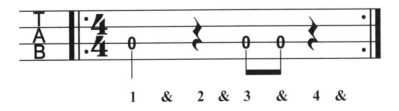

In example 2 you will play on the 1 count followed by three up beat notes played on the "&" counts. This creates a very syncopated rhythm.

Open String Bass Progression

This rock song contains all open strings. Even though you are not fretting notes you will still have to use your hand to control the strings and mute all the strings you are not playing. Make sure to play this along with the backing track. There are a lot of layers in the backing track so keep focused on your part and keep a steady bass pulse.

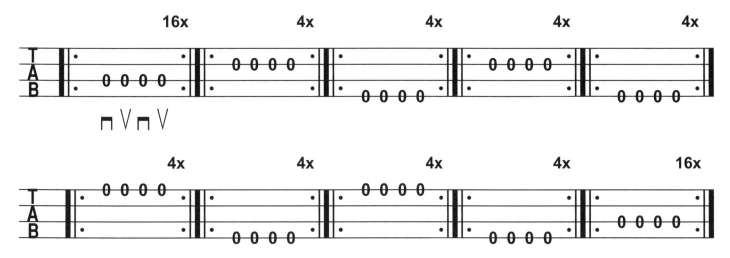

Riff Challenge

CD Track
31-34

Here are two fun riffs to challenge your fingers. Pay attention to the fingering on both hands to make sure you play the notes correctly.

Example 1

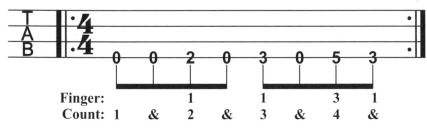

Example 2

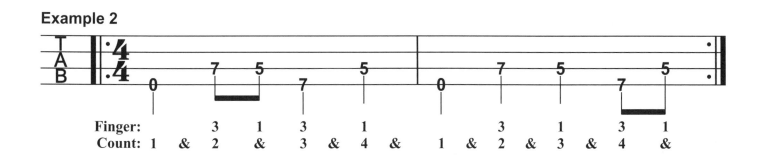

The Chromatic Scale

Intervals – The Half Step

An interval is the distance between two notes. Intervals come in different sizes gauged by the distance between the notes. If the notes are sounded in a row, it is a melodic interval. If sounded together, it is a harmonic interval. The smallest interval in music is the half step. A half step would be the distance of one fret on the bass. If you play any note and then play the note at the next fret you are playing a half step. A whole step is made up of two half steps.

Sharps and Flats

A sharp "#" means higher in pitch by a half step or one fret. A flat "b" means lower in pitch by a half step or one fret. Sharps and flats are used in music when creating chords and scales and are also referred to as accidentals.

♭ = Flat   ♯ = Sharp

The Chromatic Scale

All the music we listen to is derived from a group of 12 notes known as the Chromatic Scale. These 12 notes are all a half step (one fret) apart. There are two natural half steps in music: B to C, and E to F. There will not be a sharp or a flat between these notes. Study and memorize the Chromatic Scale below:

Natural Half Steps

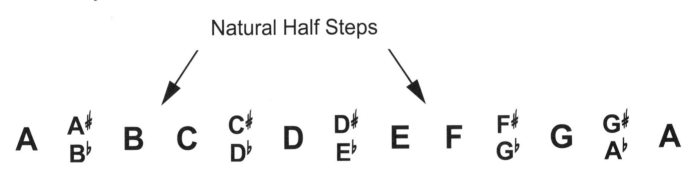

Notice that there is a common flat and sharp note, one note with two different names such as A♯/B♭. This is because if you start with an A note and raised it a half step it would be called A♯. If you start with a B note and lower it a half step it would be called B♭. Same note, different name. These are called Enharmonic notes.

MUSIC ASSIGNMENT

Write out the chromatic scale on a piece of paper starting from A and going back to A. Be sure to put the enharmonic sharps and flats on the paper. Next if you feel courageous, try writing it backwards from A to A. The better you have this memorized, the easier you will be able to follow this book.

Notes in the First Position

It's important to learn the names of the notes on your bass so you can communicate with other musicians effectively. The first position is considered the first four frets of the bass. Starting with the names of the open strings you will use the chromatic scale to learn all the notes on your bass.

Start with the 4th string open E and go up the chromatic scale from there: F first fret, F♯ second fret, G third fret, G♯ fourth fret. Next, do this same process on the other three strings. It is important to practice each string without looking and memorize the note names.

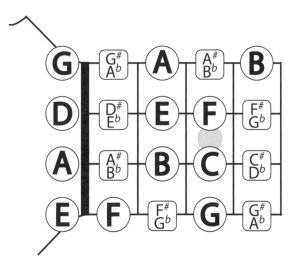

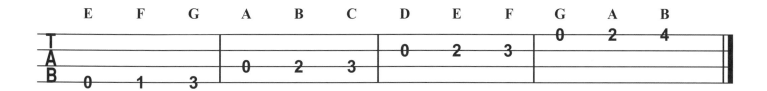

MUSIC ASSIGNMENT

Use the chromatic scale to learn the names all the way up each string. This will be a great way to better understand your instrument.

5ths

5ths are commonly used in bass lines. They are created using the root note and 5th degree of a major scale. There are five shapes that you will learn starting on the 4th, 3rd and 2nd strings. When playing the root 4th, 3rd and 2nd shapes, you will use your first and third fingers and the first finger will always be the name or root note. These are movable shapes and can be played anywhere across the neck.

The open 4th and 3rd shapes are played using your first finger and the open string will give the shape its name. Since these are open position shapes they are not moveable. Play the 5ths below:

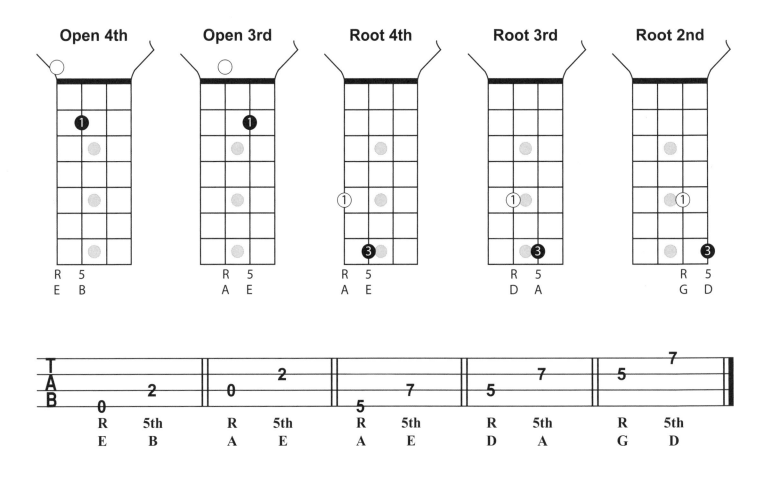

MUSIC ASSIGNMENT

Take the 5th shapes and move them around the neck to different frets. Make sure that you know the note played with your first finger will be the root note. Call out the name of each root note as you play these across the neck.

Applying 5ths

CD Track

36-38

Rock Climbing

Here is a bass line that will show you how to apply 5ths in a bass line. Notice how they follow the chord change. Many times the bass line will coordinate with the chord changes in this fashion.

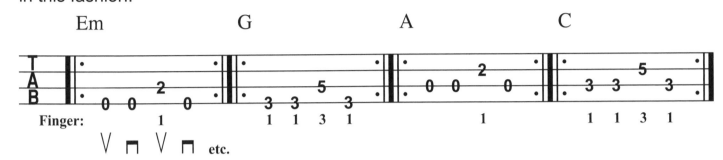

MUSIC ASSIGNMENT

Play the bass line with the backing track to create a full band sound. Concentrate on where the changes are, this will help you develop a great ear for music.

Single Note Riff

CD Track

39

The Mission

Play the last two notes of each measure quickly to get the proper rhythm.

Learn Bass 1 - Quiz 2
Once you complete this section go to RockHouseSchool.com and take the quiz to track your progress. You will receive an email with your results and suggestions.

How to Read a Scale Diagram

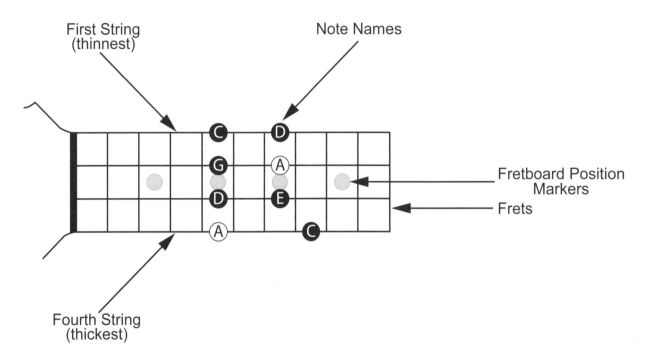

First String
(thinnest)

Note Names

Fretboard Position
Markers

Frets

Fourth String
(thickest)

Notice how the diagram above is a mirror image of the bass neck. Below see how this scale pattern looks on the bass. In the diagram above the top line is the thinnest string and the bottom is the thickest string like a tab staff.

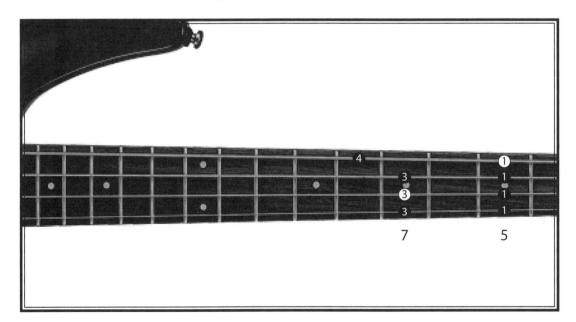

Minor Pentatonic Scale

First Position Key of "A"

SCALE PROFESSOR

Minor pentatonic scales are the most widely used scales in rock and blues music. This is a five note scale, which means that it repeats after five notes back to the beginning note (root note) in a circle-type fashion. The notes of the A minor pentatonic scale are A – C – D – E – G, then it repeats back to A. Notice that the A notes (or root notes) are in white.

Scales are your alphabet for creating bass lines and melodies. Just like you learned your alphabet in school and then expanded into words, sentences and complete stories you will learn scales for bass then expand to melodies, bass lines and complete songs. Practice this scale with a metronome using whole, half and quarter notes.

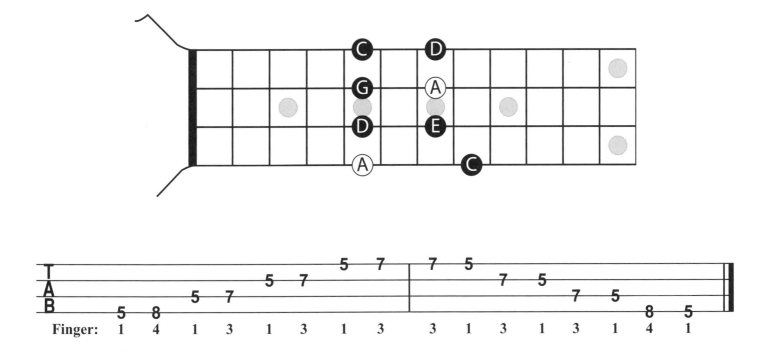

MUSIC ASSIGNMENT

After you can play this scale easily forwards and backwards, play through it, mix the notes up and see how the notes fit together perfectly. Think of this scale as a creative tool not just a group of notes forming a scale. You can even create your own bass lines within the confines of the scale notes by mixing the order and listening for interesting combinations.

Minor Pentatonic Single Note Pattern

CD Track
41

This doubling pattern comes directly from the first minor pentatonic scale. This is a great exercise to help develop the coordination of your hands and help you use the scale in a creative manner.

As you play through the scale the pattern will be to double the 3rd and 2nd strings going forward and backwards. Be sure to use alternate plucking consistently and build up your speed gradually. I recommend using a metronome to help gauge your progress.

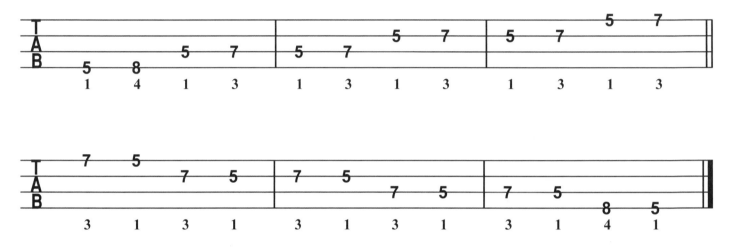

MUSIC ASSIGNMENT

Be sure to tap your foot along with the pattern to get your body clock ticking and really feel the pattern. Start by playing this pattern as quarter notes giving each note beat. Next, play each note in eighth note timing playing two notes for each beat.

Practice Tips

- Make sure to review previous lessons. A good idea is to review the past songs as a warm up before you start your new lesson.

- Use a metronome when practicing. Always start at a slow speed and increase your tempo once you can play the speed you are at comfortably.

- Record yourself if you have the capacity. When you listen back you will be more objective to any inconsistencies. Learn to be your own biggest critic.

Complete Song Progression

Clockwork

In this lesson you will learn a complete bass song progression in eighth note timing. Notice how many of the notes come from the minor pentatonic scale you just learned. Use consistent alternate plucking and build speed gradually.

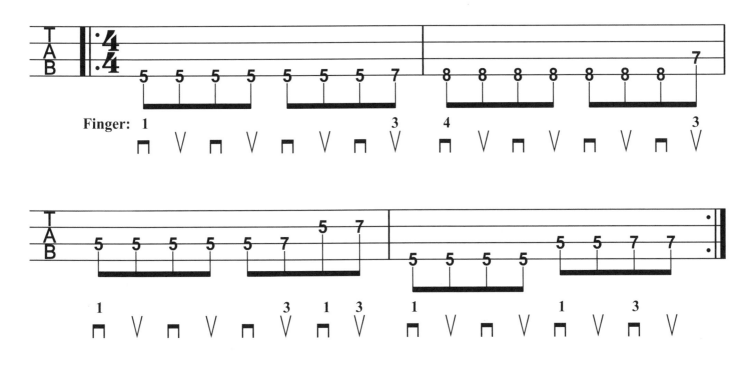

Minor Pentatonic Scale

CD Track
45-46

Positions 2 & 3

With the first minor pentatonic scale in the key of "A" you learned the names of the five notes that make this scale: A, C, D, E and G. The word pentatonic is "penta" meaning five and "tonic" meaning first note. In this lesson you'll learn the 2nd and 3rd positions of this scale. These are the same exact notes played at different places on the neck.

When learning scales a great way to memorize them is to find the finger pattern (the fingers you use on each string). The finger pattern for the second position scale is 2 – 4, 1 – 4, 1 – 4, 1 – 3 always keep your fingers in a one finger per fret alignment. Play through this position and get familiar with the pattern. Again, notice that the root notes are in white.

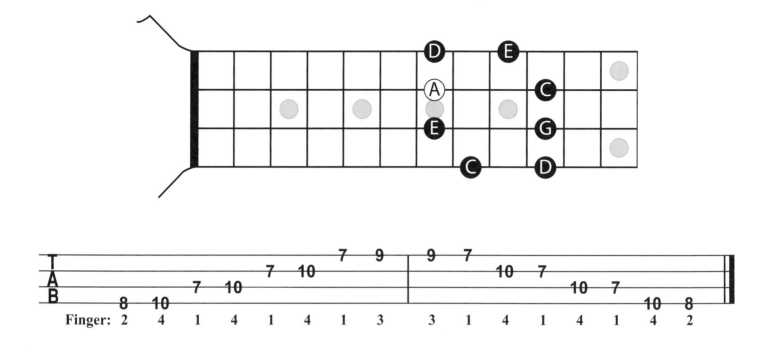

The 3rd scale position starts on the 10th fret, and the finger pattern is 1 – 3, 1 – 3, 1 – 3, 1 – 4. The tricky part here is on the 1st string you have to shift down to the 9th fret to get the first note, then stretch your fourth finger to the 12th fret to get the second note.

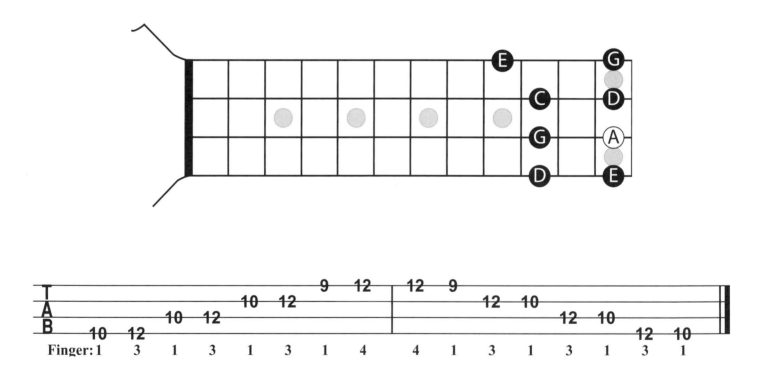

Make sure to use alternate plucking as you build up speed with these scales. Memorize the patterns so that you could play them easily and effectively. Also try to memorize the locations of the root notes within the scale patterns. In the coming lessons I will show you patterns that use these scales, so get excited!

Minor Pentatonic Single Note Pattern

CD Track 47-48

Positions 2 & 3

Take the double pattern you learned earlier and apply it to the scales in the previous lesson. Double the notes on the 2nd and 3rd strings going forward and backwards through each scale. Play the 2nd scale position below:

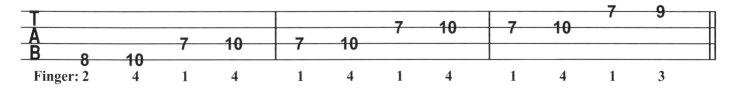

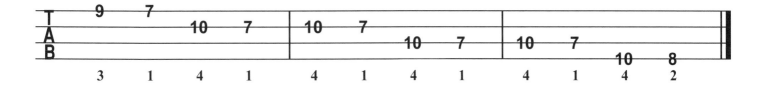

Next apply this pattern to the 3rd scale position, starting on the 10th fret.

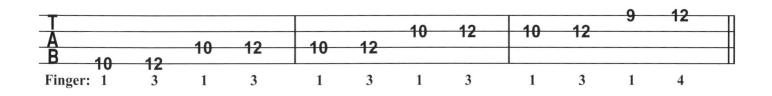

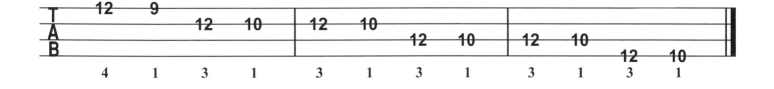

MUSIC ASSIGNMENT

Once you're comfortable with this pattern, practice along with a metronome to gauge your progress. Start at a slow tempo and increase the tempo each time you practice. Keep clean technique, plucking each note clear and distinct, while alternating consistently. To make this pattern more challenging pluck each note twice as you play through the pattern sequence.

Blues Riff Rhythm

The following is a single note blues riff rhythm. There are many times in music where a rhythm for a song will be constructed using single notes played with the bass and the guitar together. This is a common rhythm so it should sound familiar. Be sure to play this over the guitar and drum backing track.

E

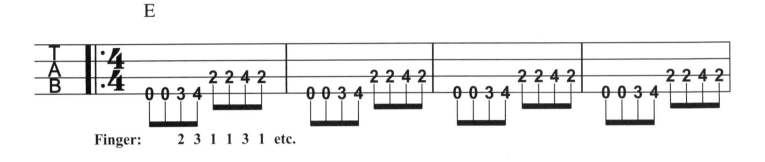

Finger: 2 3 1 1 3 1 etc.

A   E

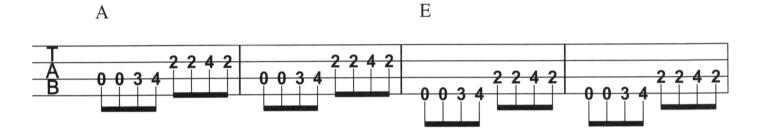

B   A   E

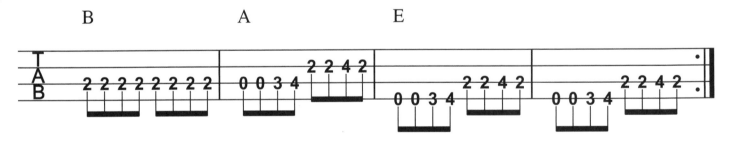

MUSIC ASSIGNMENT

This rhythm can be played with the shuffle feel that you learned in the Blues Progression lesson. Below are the first few measures with the shuffle feel rhythm to get you started:

E

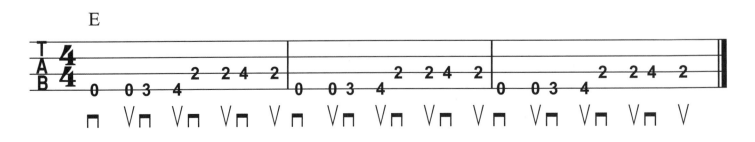

Bass Power Chords

CHORD PROFESSOR

Chords are not just for guitar players. Bass players can use chords to create big sounding bass lines. Let's start with a basic two note power chord. This chord is also known as a "5 chord" because the two notes that make the chord are the root and the 5th scale degree above that. These are the same two notes that you learned in the lesson on 5ths only to make a chord you will hit both notes together. You can strum the chords with your thumb in a downward motion or use your index and middle fingers. The two chords you will learn have the lowest note as the root note on the 3rd and 2nd strings.

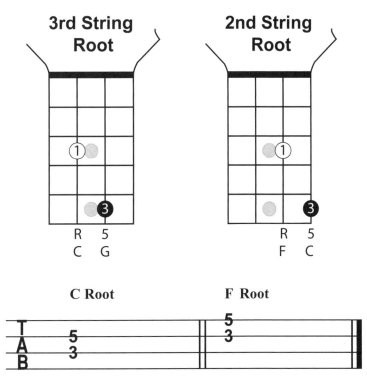

These two chords can be played on any fret on the neck, however, they change names as they are moved. Follow the chart to see what the name of each chord is when moved to different frets on the neck.

	2nd String Root											
Name -	E♭5	E5	F5	F♯5	G5	G♯5	A5	A♯5	B5	C5	C♯5	D5
Fret -	1	2	3	4	5	6	7	8	9	10	11	12
Name -	B♭5	B5	C5	C♯5	D5	D♯5	E5	F5	F♯5	G5	G♯5	A5
	3rd String Root											

Applying Power Chords

Double Trouble

Here is a half note bass line that contains power chords. Make sure to hit both notes together in one swift motion.

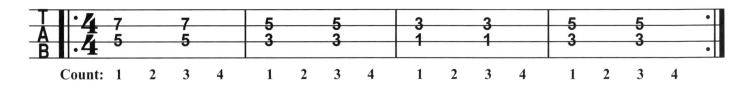

Triplets

Eighth and sixteenth notes subdivide a beat in half and quarters. These are even number breakdowns of 2 and 4. Triplets subdivide a beat into threes. For every one beat, you're going to play three notes. Count triplets like this:

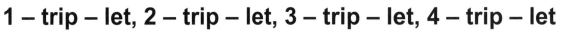

Next play the open 4th E string in triplets following the tablature below and feel the triplet timing:

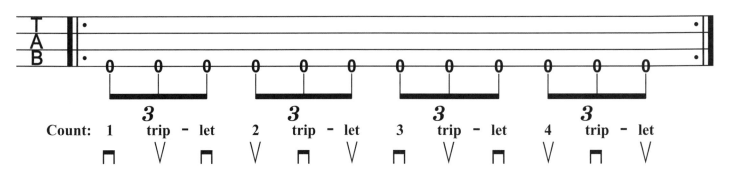

Triplet Pattern

Here is a triplet pattern applied to the first three minor pentatonic scales. This pattern goes up three notes from each degree of the scale. Below I've outlined the first two strings so you can get familiar with the pattern:

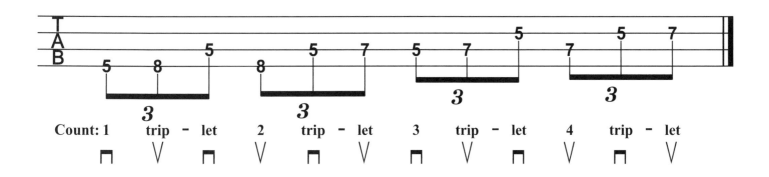

Now play the triplet lead pattern with the first three minor pentatonic scales:

1st Position

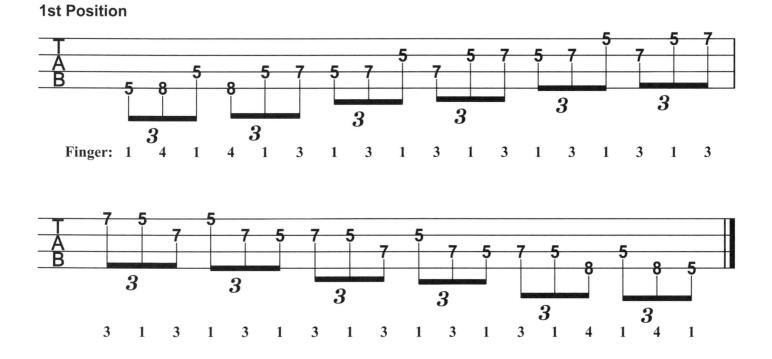

2nd Position

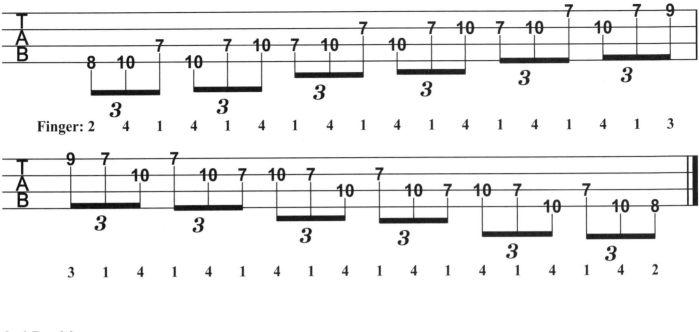

Finger: 2 4 1 4 1 4 1 4 1 4 1 4 1 4 1 4 1 3

3 1 4 1 4 1 4 1 4 1 4 1 4 1 4 1 4 2

3rd Position

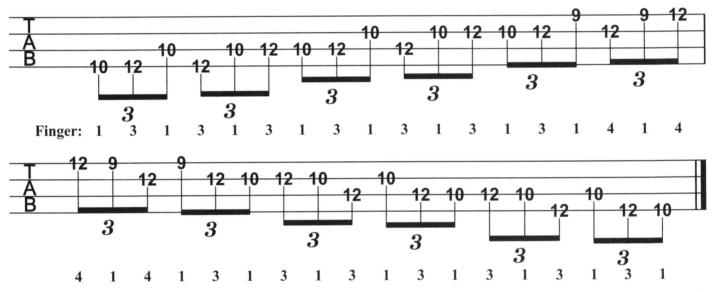

Finger: 1 3 1 3 1 3 1 3 1 3 1 3 1 3 1 4 1 4

4 1 4 1 3 1 3 1 3 1 3 1 3 1 3 1 3 1

MUSIC ASSIGNMENT

Vary this pattern and play each note of this triplet pattern two times. Then transpose this pattern forwards and backwards with all three scale positions.

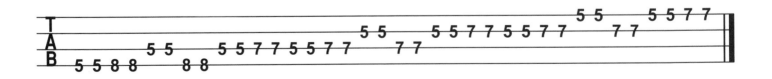

Staccato

Staccato by definition means short and detached. A note separated by silence. To attain this you must use both hands to mute the sound. With your fretting hand you simply lift the pressure off a note and with your plucking hand use the side of your hand to touch the strings as they come off the bridge. Notes that are to be played with staccato will have a dot placed over the note. Play the following notes using the staccato technique.

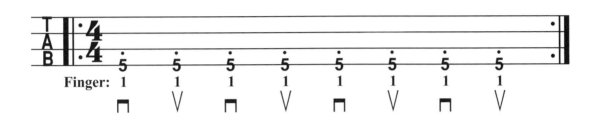

Staccato Groove

CD Track
59-60

Below is a staccato groove bass progression. Make sure to use the mute technique and also lift the pressure off each note to get the staccato sound.

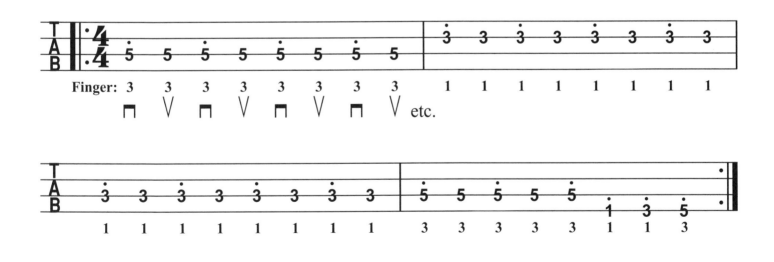

The Major Scale

Key of "G"

SCALE PROFESSOR

The major scale is the mother of all music. All scales and chords are created by altering this scale and isolating certain notes within them. The first note of the scale is the name of the key or root note. This is a G major scale starting with a G note on the 4th string 3rd fret. Pay close attention to the fingering and keep your fingers lined up, one finger per fret.

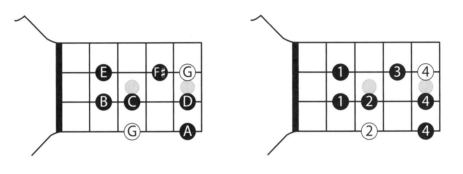

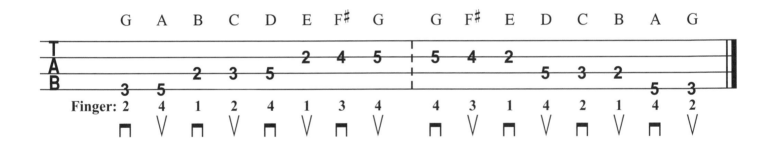

Learn Bass 1 - Quiz 3

Once you complete this section go to RockHouseSchool.com and take the quiz to track your progress. You will receive an email with your results and suggestions.

Major Triads

A triad is the three notes that make a chord. Many bass lines are written using triad patterns. In this lesson you will learn a common major triad pattern. These are movable triad patterns and by just playing the same pattern at other frets you will change keys. Often when playing with a guitar or keyboard player you can follow the chords they play with the triad of the same key. This is a great way to begin creating bass lines.

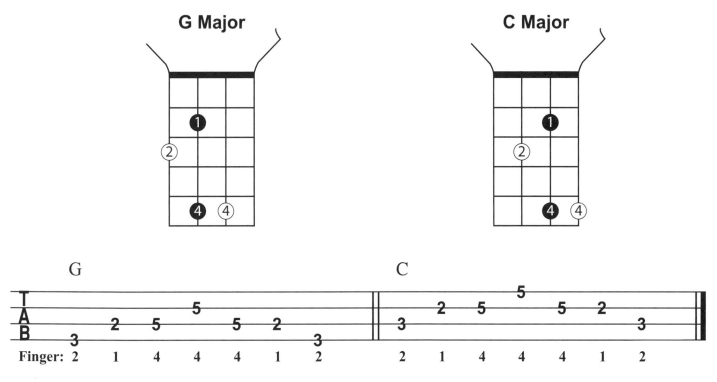

Music Assignment

Take the triad shapes from this lesson and move them around the neck. You need to become familiar playing these anywhere on the neck. Remember that the first note is the name of the triad.

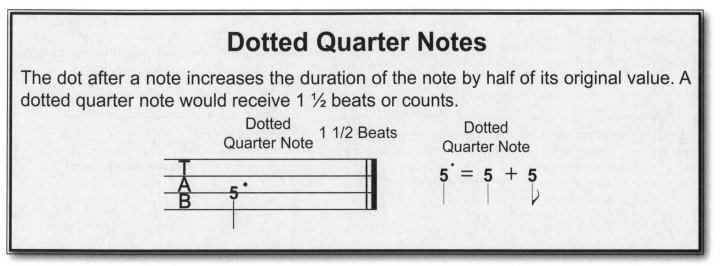

Dotted Quarter Notes

The dot after a note increases the duration of the note by half of its original value. A dotted quarter note would receive 1 ½ beats or counts.

41

Major Triad Progression

Cherry Sky

Let's put the major triads into a progression and form a bass line. The following is a four chord progression formed with the chords G, C, A and D. You will play major triads for these four chords within this bass line.

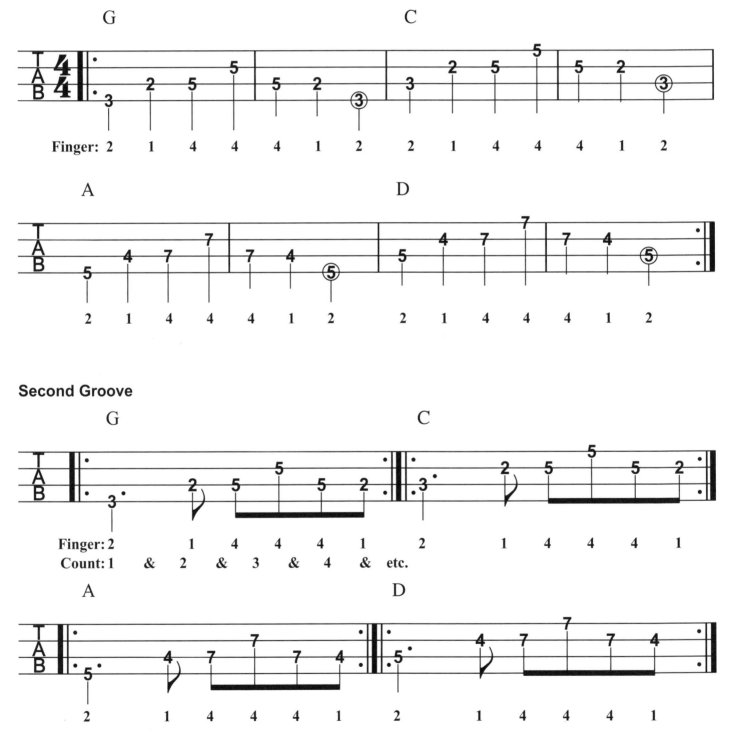

Minor Triads

A minor triad is similar to the major triads you learned only they contain the three notes that form a minor chord. These patterns are also movable and can be played in other keys by moving them to different frets across the neck. Get familiar with these minor triads.

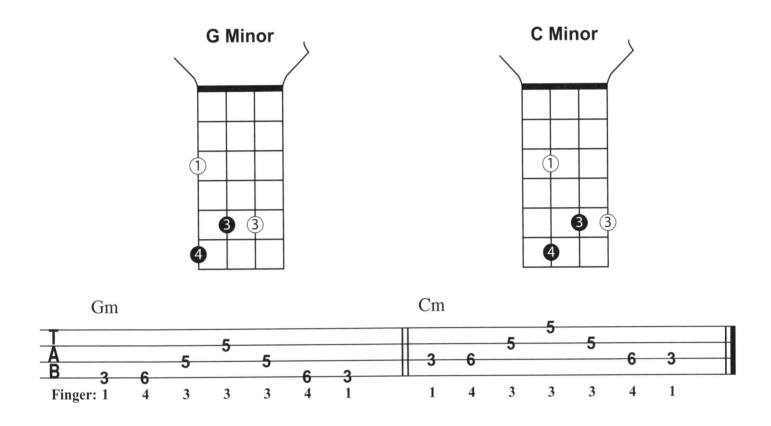

MUSIC ASSIGNMENT

Take the triad shapes from this lesson and move them around the neck. You need to become familiar playing them anywhere on the neck. Remember that the first note is the name of the triad key.

Minor Triad Progression

Unbreakable

Let's put the minor triads into a progression and form a bass line. You will use the same four chord progression from the major triads formed with the G, C, A and D chords. You will play minor triads for these four chords within this bass line. Make sure to play this over the band backing track.

First Groove

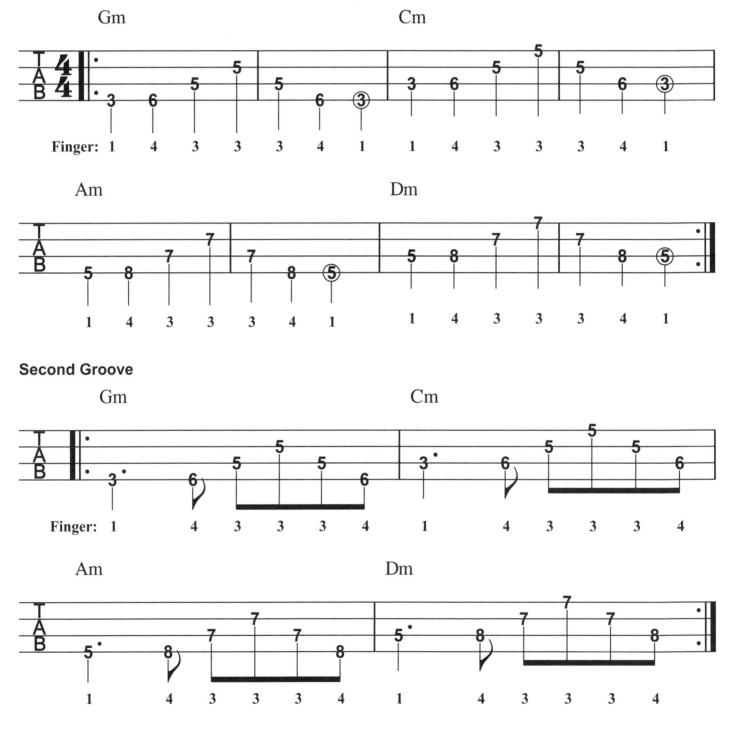

Second Groove

Major & Minor Triads

A Spell on Me

Many times you will combine both major and minor triads to form a bass line. The following is a great example of this in a two part song progression. This first section is a verse and the second section is the chorus. Make sure to play this along with the backing track after you can play it up to speed.

Part 1

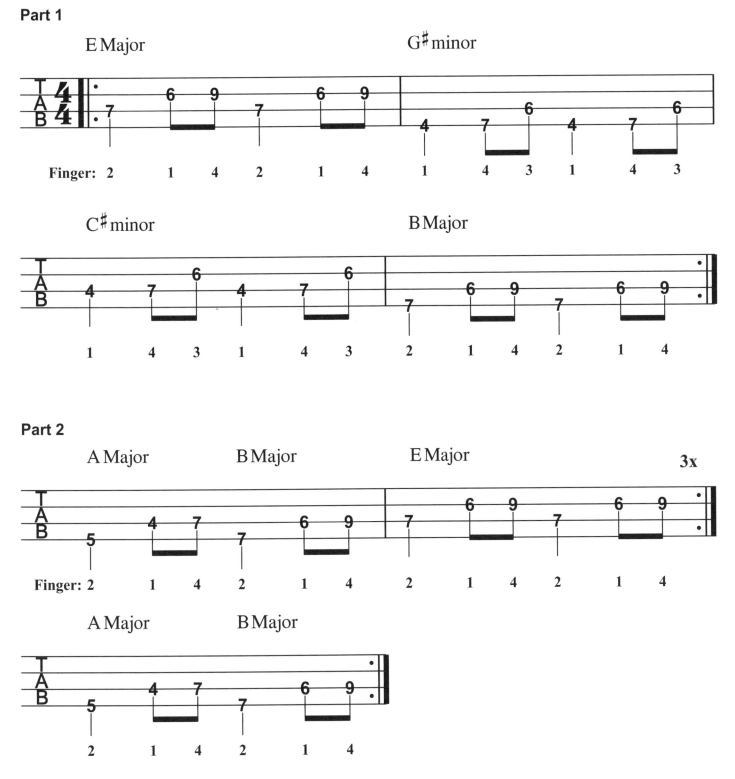

Part 2

Octaves

Octaves are a common intervallic technique used in all genres of music. Octaves are formed by taking a root note and finding the same root note 8 scale degrees higher creating a higher pitched root note. There are a few shapes that are most characteristic that I am going to show you. These shapes incorporate a string skip where you have to play a note two strings away. Many players use octaves in bass lines as a technique. Play through the following octave shapes and move them around the neck to different frets.

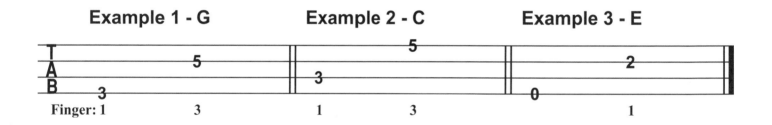

Example 1 - G   **Example 2 - C**   **Example 3 - E**

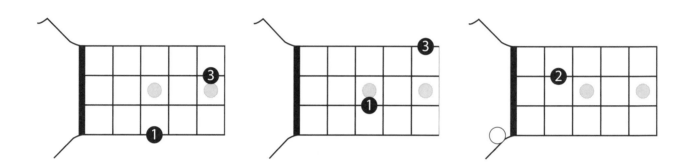

MUSIC ASSIGNMENT

Start at the 2nd fret and move these patterns one fret at a time all the way up and down the neck. It's important to be comfortable playing these octaves anywhere on the neck so you can use them to play songs.

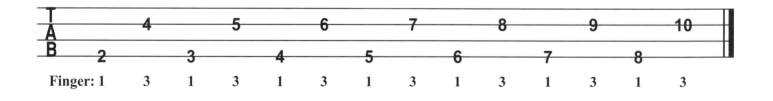

Octave Rock Progression

The tablature notes are spaced to help you with the timing. Pay close attention to the plucking, the pattern repeats but is not consistent alternate plucking.

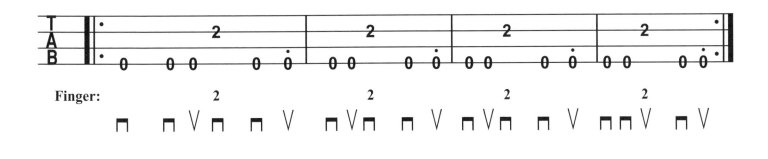

Applying Octaves

The Chase

Here is an example of how you can use octaves to create a bass line. The chord changes here are G – F – Bb – C. For this song the octave shapes will be played with the first and fourth fingers, this is a common fingering variation. Make sure to use alternate plucking consistently throughout this bass line.

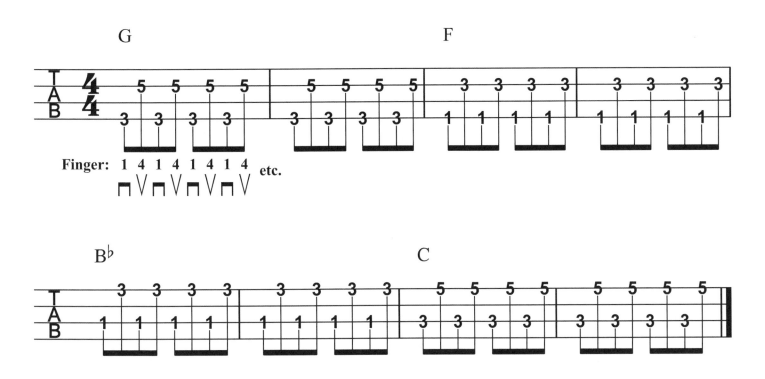

Minor Pentatonic Scale

Positions 4 & 5

Up to now you've learned three minor pentatonic scale patterns in the key of "A." Now it's time to learn the last two. The 4th scale position starts on the 12th fret with your first finger. Play through this scale position below:

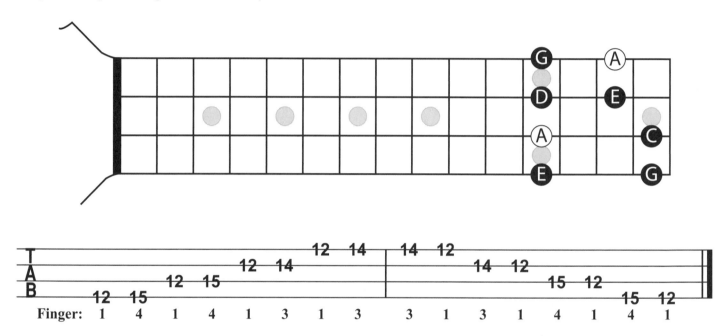

The 5th scale position starts on the 3rd fret with your second finger. This pattern is pretty easy to memorize, play through the this scale below:

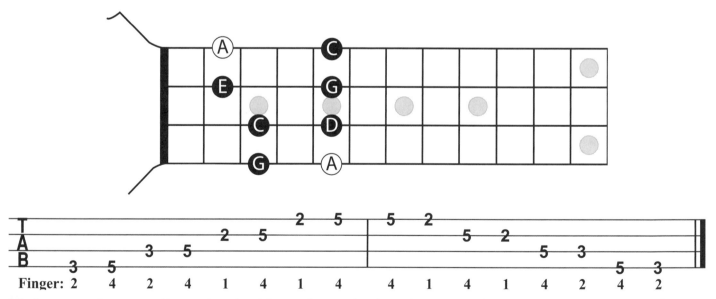

Make sure to use alternate plucking when playing these scales and memorize the finger patterns. Now you have all five minor pentatonic scale patterns in the key of "A." All of these patterns have the same notes, A – C – D – E and G played at different spots across the neck. Once you have these five patterns memorized you'll be able to change keys by just moving these scale patterns up or down the neck.

Minor Pentatonic Triplet Pattern

Positions 4 & 5

Below is the triplet pattern transposed to the 4th and 5th position minor pentatonic scale. Pay attention to your hand position and keep the bass neck up at a 30 degree angle.

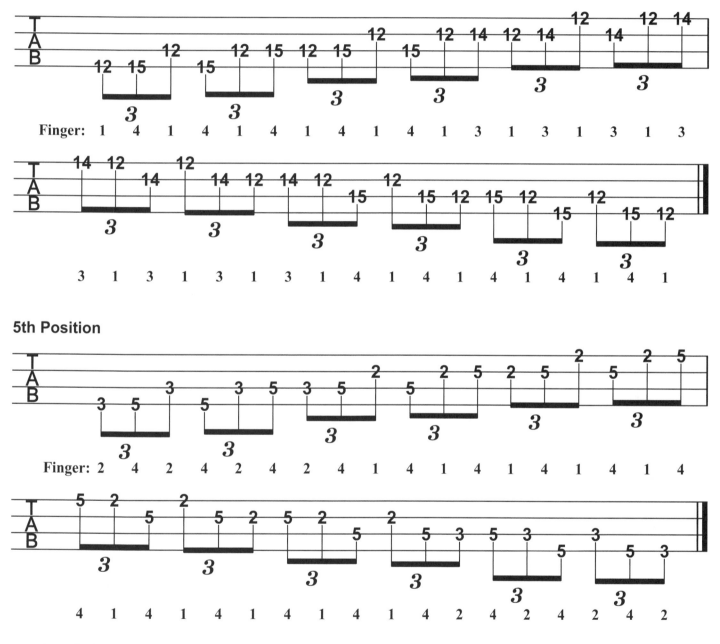

MUSIC ASSIGNMENT

Scales are meant to be used to create bass lines and melodies. After you play the scales forward and backward, try to mix the notes up and create your own patterns. This is how you begin creating your own style.

Finger Flexing #2

Here is another exercise that will help develop the coordination of both hands. In this exercise, there's a wide stretch to help open up your hand's reach to play harder passages.

The fret pattern that you are going to use is 1 – 4 – 3 – 4, using alternate plucking. Use the same finger as fret when you play this exercise and line your fingers up in a one finger per fret manner.

Hold your first finger down on each string, this will help to open up your hand and develop a reach while building coordination of both hands. Repeat each measure four times and use alternate plucking. Do the same pattern on all four strings.

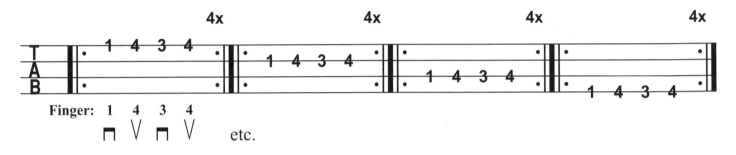

Build up speed gradually. This is a great time to use a metronome to help you gauge your progress. Increase the speed a notch every day to effectively improve your skill.

MUSIC ASSIGNMENT

Once you feel comfortable playing this pattern across all four strings, do the same pattern doubling each note. The pattern would look like this:

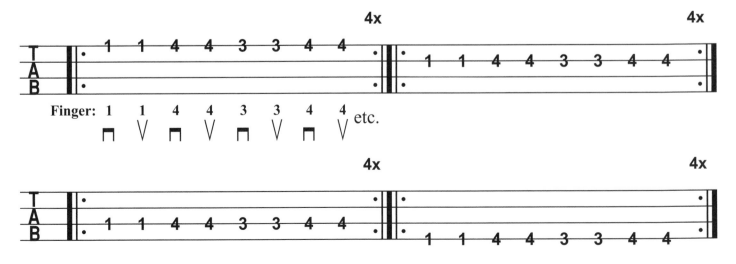

Using a Pick

Although using your fingers to pick the strings is the recommended technique there are times you may want to use a pick to get a different sound. You should hold the pick between your index finger and thumb with the point of the pick facing toward the strings.

Center the pick on the index finger of your right hand.

Bring your thumb down on top of the pick. Pinch your thumb and finger together and leave just the tip of the pick showing.

Leave your hand open and your other fingers relaxed (don't make a fist). Your thumb and finger should be placed in the center of the pick, grasping it firmly to give you good control.

Palm Muting

You learned how to use the mute technique to stop the sound completely. Another common way this technique is played is to lightly touch your picking hand against the strings just as they come off the bridge. Make sure not to go too far from the bridge because this will deaden the note completely. Make the notes come out slightly deadened but so you can still hear the pitch of each note. This is used in many genres of music and often in heavy rock music. Play the open 4th string on the next page using a pick to get familiar with this muting technique. Notice the "p.m." followed by a dotted line that indicates palm muting on the staff.

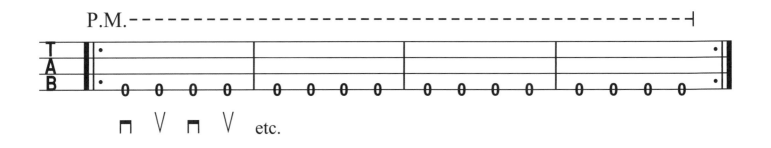

П V П V etc.

Applying the Mute Technique

Rockit Center

Here is a simple bass line to apply the muting technique. All the notes are on the E and A strings so you can keep a consistent mute on those strings for the entire progression. Use the band backing track to get the full band sensation.

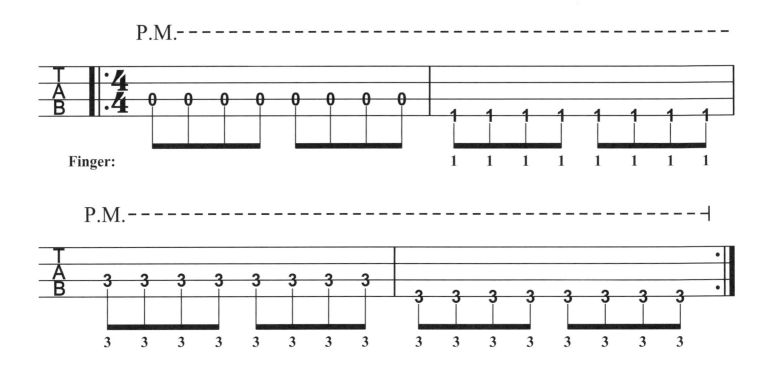

MUSIC ASSIGNMENT

Apply the muting technique used in this lesson to some of the bass lines you have learned earlier in the book. Adding the mute technique will give each progression a new dynamic sound.

Basic Slap & Pop Technique

CD Track
89-90

Slap and pop is a popular bass plucking technique used in many genres of music. For the slap, make sure to use the side of your thumb slapping the bass string to sound a note. It is a very quick movement and the thumb should not stay on the string. The higher notes are snapped or popped to sound the note. Place your middle finger of the plucking hand under the string and snap it up to generate the sound. Both the slap and pop are very percussive techniques and should be hit and snapped quick and hard.

Slap

Let's start with the slap technique, with the side of your thumb slap your thumb against the 4th string right after the end of the neck as shown in the diagram. Make sure to bounce your thumb off the string right after it hits to allow the note to ring. Play a series of slaps on the 4th string to get familiar with the technique.

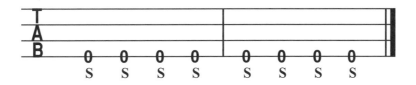

Pop

Now let's go through the pop technique. On your plucking hand, bend your index finger in a hook shape and place it under the 1st string. Pull your hand up keeping it in a locked position. Play a series of pops on the 1st string to get familiar with this technique.

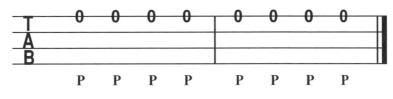

Slap & Pop Exercise

In this example you will slap the open E string and pop the open G string. Once you have the bass line so you can play it smoothly play it along with the backing track.

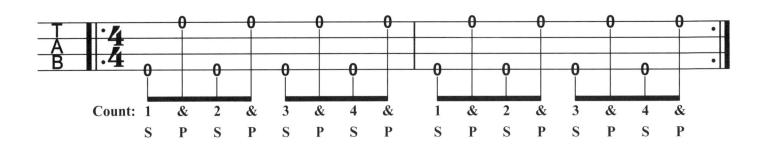

Applying the Slap & Pop Technique

Now let's apply the slap & pop technique into a song. Below is a simple song that will incorporate three octave shapes. Play each separately first then put them together with the backing track. This song is played with a swing or shuffle feel so pay close attention to the backing track for the rhythms timing.

Example 1

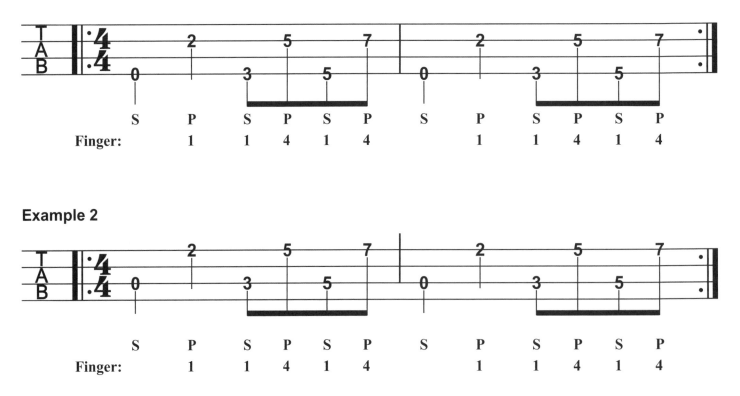

Example 2

Warm Up Exercises

In this lesson you will learn a warm up routine, great to use when you first start your playing session. A good warm up routine is essential to becoming a good bass player. Once you learn each pattern, continue to play them all the way up the neck using alternate plucking.

Example 1

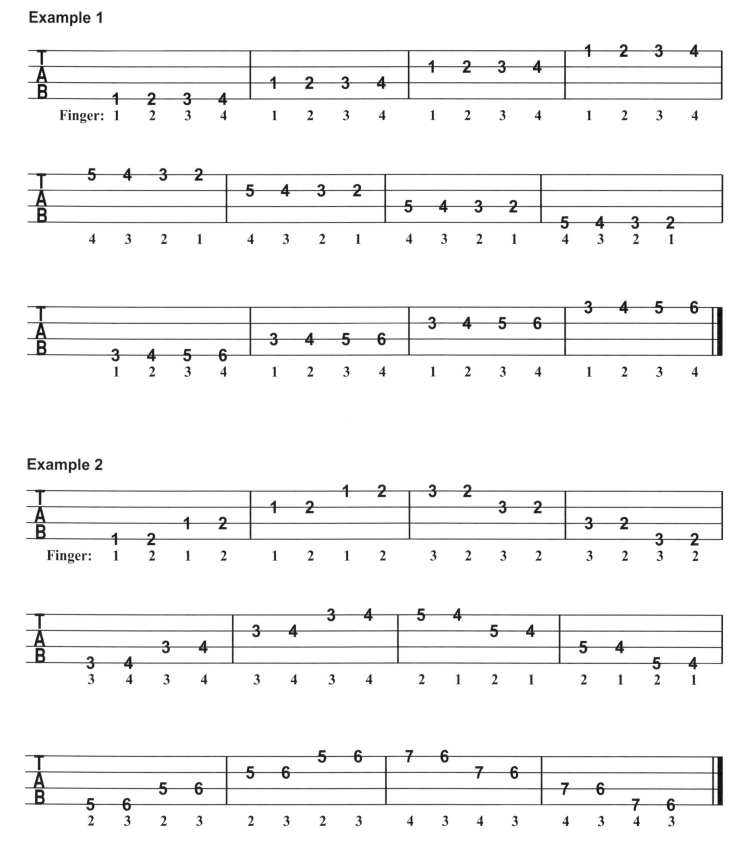

Heavy Bass Progression

This is a simple but effective bass line. The timing is eighth notes until the last two notes which are quarter notes. The last two notes are a half step apart and create a dark sound. This is common in heavy rock or metal music. Make sure to use alternate plucking and play along with the backing track to create a full band sound.

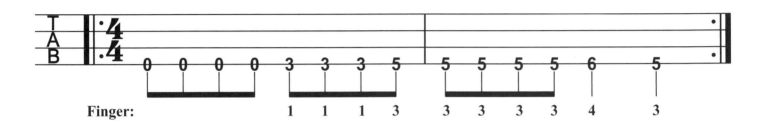

Single Note Riff Rhythm

This is a 12 bar blues rhythm with a rock feel. I have placed the chord changes above the staff to help you follow the progression. The guitar follows the same pattern with the bass in unison creating a full driving sound.

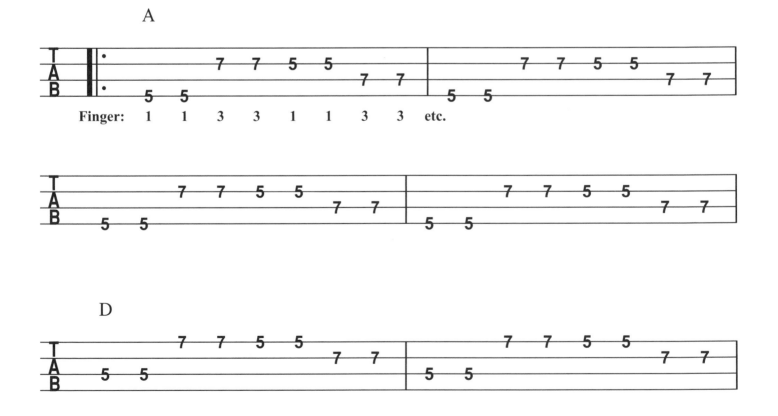

A

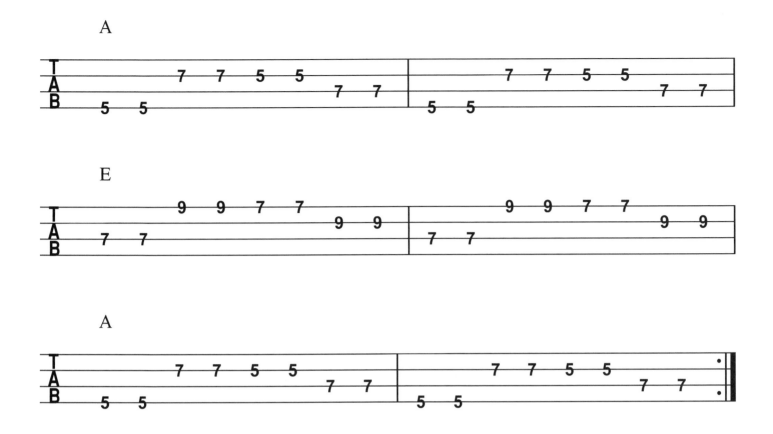

E

A

Learn Bass 1 - Quiz 4

Congratulations you've made it to the end of Book 1! Go to RockHouseSchool. com and take the quiz to track your progress. You will receive an email with your results and an official Rock House Method "Certificate of Completion" when you pass.

Appendix

Word Search

Go to RockHouseSchool.com to get the solution to this word search.

```
T M E U Y J R D L S C L M V H M P U N D R I H T S
O L A D A W G A Z G F J O X G N J O X G Y F C Q Z
T X O J I T C E D Y F Y D K L P I I T E N O F L A
I N C U O D R H Q J Z R F I N S B B M O B B D F R
U W T R L R G E J S C I J F S A I J I L A M Z K N
P P A W M C P N V A K D B E I X K B E D S M A M X
K A V I Y V N I A Q P O R X H R C B D N S L R R G
M C E E V T S H S J A G H A R S O S N B J N T O K
B S T C S S K C N D O F O J Y I R X I G V H Q G N
L O Y I P R D A K R F L Z Z W J B L C I W S I W X
N W D O Q P N M P I C E P G H W U R E X J T S I N
J I Y Q H X J J F P S C L O C A C J I F B Z E R H
W Q T J D M N T O L J S T A P T A J X D B W U U G
Q S Q T D F H I G D E T E Y C J B E M H G V L N U
P M A H L X Y U E L R G H T W S G R P Q L E B A D
K F P Z J W B J A V V L T R I P L E T Y B L Y X A
F C H M H U N X V Y A Y K C D G U I Q K U L E E N
J F C Y R D Y H T O O R K O U H Q A Y O D E B T G
X M Q I A W O B H J D H B M U T E B L K W K E C D
O V V I H R G U Y A L V M X R U Q I W X N J B T U
H I R A C L V A W Y B A C B P D S H U F Z H V J D
O T E Z J S D C E V O Z P A A P S Y M D X Z M E D
W U T Z R K B U E I E G U T M L W Q L S H E M X H
V X S P W E C G S M I N O R A G A D K N P Q F J M
V P S G N O Z M A V B Q R P W B K B Q L N C T N F
```

Search Words:

- BASS
- BLUES
- BRIDGE
- FIFTH
- MACHINE HEAD
- MAJOR
- MINOR
- MUTE

- NOTE
- OCTAVE
- POP
- PROGRESSION
- RIFF
- ROCK
- SCALE
- SLAP

- THIRD
- TRIAD
- TRIPLET

Musical Words

Action – Height of the strings from the fret board to the string itself.

Beat – The regular pulse of music which may be dictated by a metronome, or by the accents in music.

Bridge – The bridge is located on the body of the bass and transfers sound from the strings to the body of the bass. This is held in place by screws or string tension.

Body – The main section of the instrument where the bridge and tailpiece are located.

Fretboard or Fingerboard – The area on top of the neck that you press the string upon to create a note or frequency.

Flat – An accidental symbol placed to the left of a note, indicating that its pitch should be lowered by a half step.

Fret – The metal bars along your fretboard that separate the notes on the neck.

Headstock – Top of the instrument where the tuners or machine heads are located.

Interval – The distance between two pitches.

Machine Head – A device to control the tension of the strings. With a slight turn of the machine head, the player can tighten or loosen the tension to raise or lower the pitch of the string until it is in tune.

Measure – A musical term signifying the smallest division of a song, containing a fixed number of beats, marked off by vertical lines on the staff. The distance between two bar lines on a staff.

Melody – A succession of single tones containing rhythm and pitches arranged as a musical shape.

Neck – The middle of the bass where the strings are stretched over the fretboard.

Nut – Piece of plastic or bone between the headstock and fretboard. Guides the strings from the fretboard to the tuners on the headstock.

Pickguard – Piece of material placed on the body of the bass to protect it from pick scratches.

Pickup – Device that takes the string vibration that you create and transform it into an electronic signal. This signal it then used in amplifiers to boost the sound.

Pop – A plucking technique where you put a finger under the string and pull or snap upward to sound the note. Usually played with the index or middle fingers on the higher strings.

Saddles – Piece on the bridge that holds the string in place.

Scale – A series of notes in ascending or descending order that presents the pitches of a key or mode, beginning and ending on the tonic of that key or mode.

Sharp – An accidental symbol placed to the left of a note, indicating that its pitch should be raised by a half step.

Slap – The technique in which the string is being struck with the side of the thumb to sound a note. Very much like hammers on a piano strike the strings.

Tempo – The speed of the rhythm of a composition. Tempo is measured according to beats per minute.

Timing – The beat of musical rhythm. The controlled movement of music in time.

Triplet – Three notes of equal length that are to be performed in the duration of two notes of equal length.

Truss Rod – A long rod inside your bass neck used for stabilizing a wooden neck to its proper angle.

Crossword Puzzle

Go to RockHouseSchool.com to get the solution to this crossword puzzle.

Across
2. Lowers a notes pitch one half step
4. Raises a notes pitch one half step
5. Eight scale degrees above the root
7. Sounding a note by striking it with the side of your thumb
9. A device that clicks at an adjustable rate to help with timing
10. The 12 notes that make up all music
11. Type of note receiving 4 beats

Down
1. Short and detached
3. Three notes played in one beats time
6. Type of note receiving 1 beat
7. A group of notes that are in the same key
8. A symbol that tells you there will be a period of silence

Changing a String

Old bass strings may break or lose their tone and become harder to keep in tune. You might feel comfortable at first having a teacher or someone at a music store change your strings for you, but eventually you will need to know how to do it yourself. Changing the strings on a bass is not as difficult as it may seem and the best way to learn how to do this is by practicing. Bass strings are fairly expensive so it's important to get it right the first time you try to restring your bass. How often you change your strings depends entirely on how much you play your bass, but if the same strings have been on it for months, it's probably time for a new set.

Before removing the old strings from the bass, examine the way it is attached to and try to duplicate that with the new string. On some electric basses, the string may need to be threaded through a hole in the back of the body.

Follow the series of photos below for a basic description of how to change a string. Before trying it yourself, read through the quick tips for beginners on the following page.

Loosen the string.

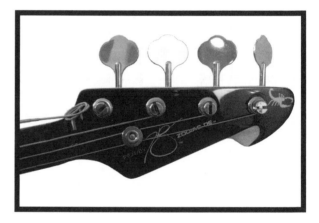

Remove the old string from the post.

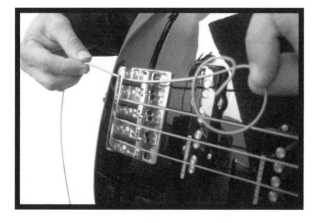

Pull the string through the bridge and discard it.

Remove the new string from the packaging and uncoil it.

Thread the end of the new string through the bridge.

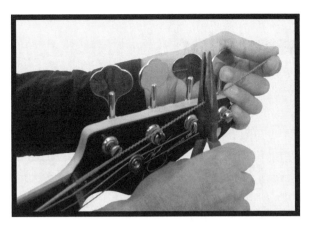

Cut the excess length from the string.

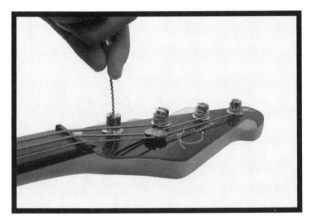

Hold the string in place just after the nut with your finger and tighten up the slack in the string with the machine head.

Carefully tighten the string and tune it to the proper pitch.

You can cut the old string off the bass but you may want to unwind it instead and save it as a spare in case you break a string later. Check to make sure you have the correct string in your hand before putting it on the bass. The strings may be color coded at the end to help you identify them.

Thread the new string through the bridge and cut the end of the string approximately three inches past the tuner you are anchoring the string to. Insert the cut end into the top of the machine head and bend the string around it. Be sure to wind the string around the tuning post in the proper direction (see photos). The string should wind around the post underneath itself to form a neat coil. Once the extra slack is taken up and the string is taught, tune it very gradually to pitch, being careful not to over tighten and accidentally break the new string. Check the ends of the string to make sure it is sitting correctly on the proper bridge saddle and space on the nut. New strings will go out of tune very quickly until they are broken in. You can gently massage the new string with your thumbs and fingers once it's on the bass, slightly stretching the string out and helping to break it in. Then retune the string and repeat this process a few times for each string.

Bass Triads

A Major

4th fr.

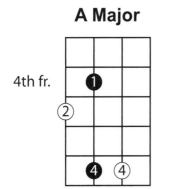

A

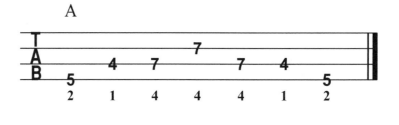

A Major

11th fr.

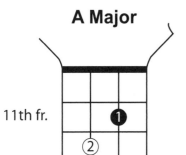

A

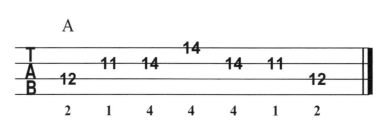

A Minor

5th fr.

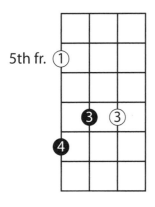

Am

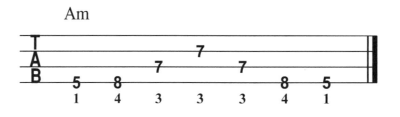

A Minor

12th fr.

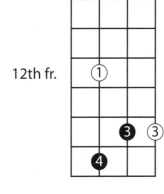

Am

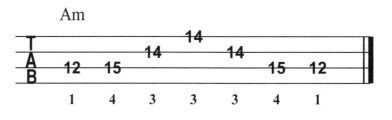

B Major

6th fr.

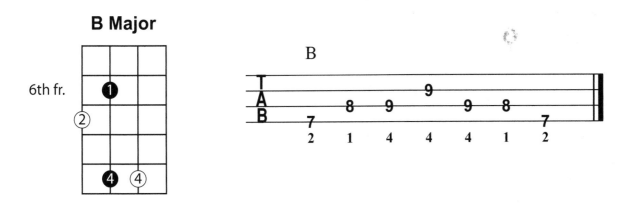

B

```
T                      9
A        8   9              9   8
B    7                         7
     2   1   4   4   4   1   2
```

B Major

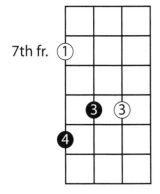

B

```
T                  4
A        1   4         4   1
B    2                     2
     2   1   4   4   4   1   2
```

B Minor

7th fr.

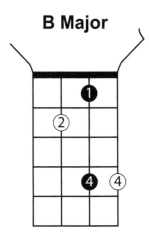

Bm

```
T                  9
A            9         9
B    7  10            10   7
     1   4   3   3   3   4   1
```

B Minor

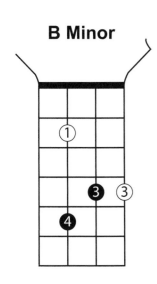

Bm

```
T                  4
A            4         4
B    2   5            5   2
     1   4   3   3   3   4   1
```

C Major

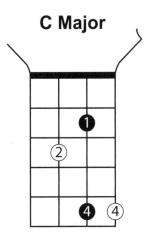

7th fr.

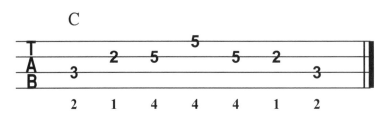

C

C Major

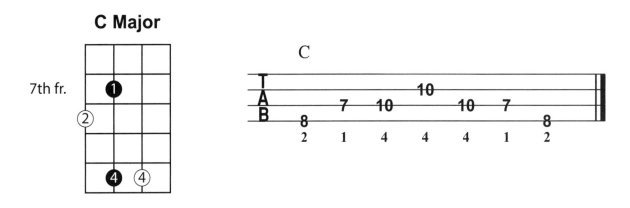

C

C Minor

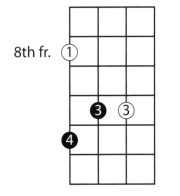

8th fr.

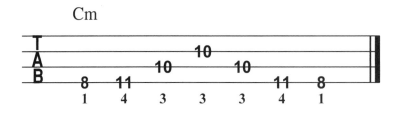

Cm

C Minor

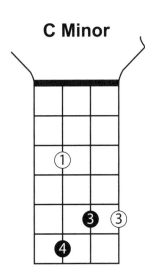

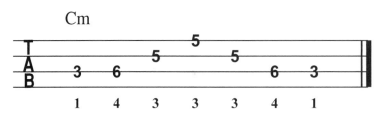

Cm

D Major

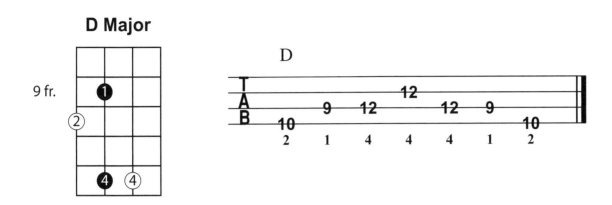

9 fr.

D

D Major

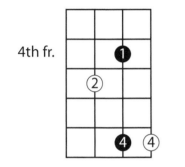

4th fr.

D

D Minor

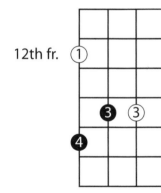

12th fr.

Dm

D Minor

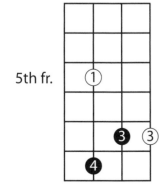

5th fr.

Dm

E Major

11th fr.

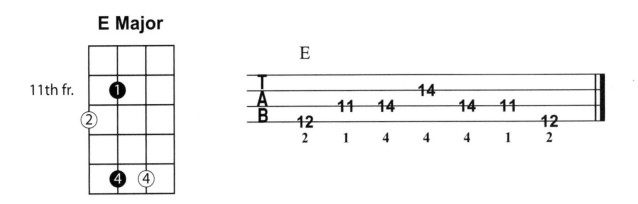

E

E Major

6th fr.

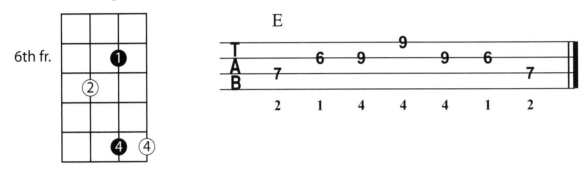

E

E Minor

12th fr.

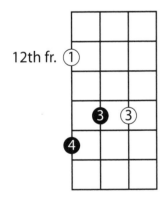

Em

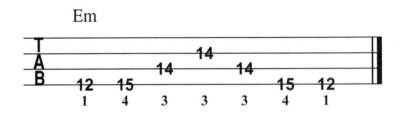

E Minor

7th fr.

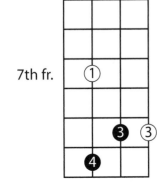

Em

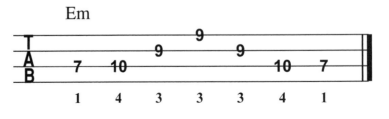

F Major

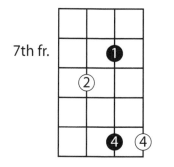

12th fr.

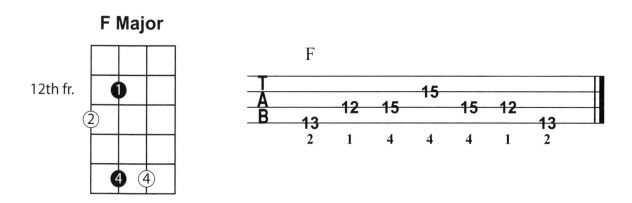

F

F Major

7th fr.

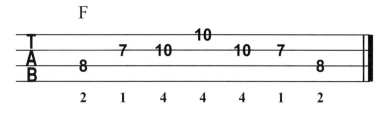

F

F Minor

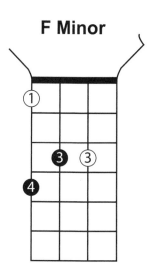

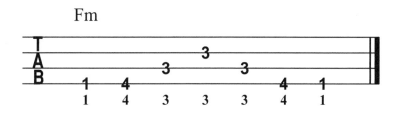

Fm

F Minor

8th fr.

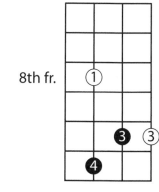

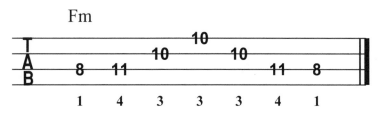

Fm

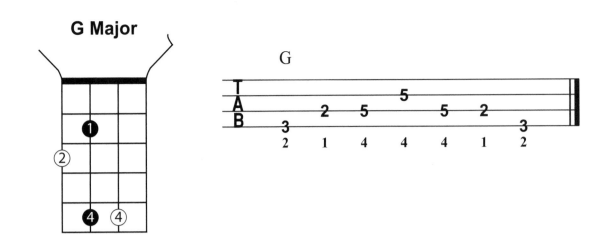

G Major

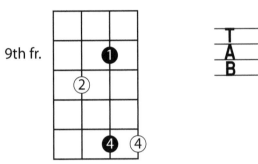

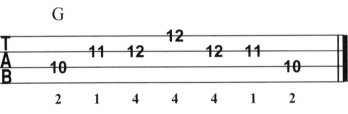

G Major

9th fr.

G Minor

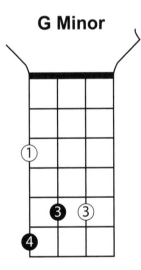

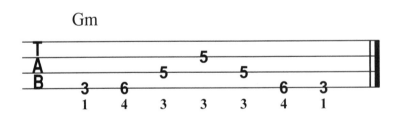

G Minor

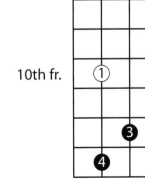

10th fr.

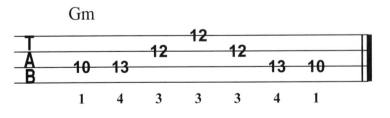

About the Author

John McCarthy
Creator of
The Rock House Method

John is the creator of The Rock House Method®, the world's leading musical instruction system. Over his 25 plus year career, he has written, produced and/or appeared in more than 100 instructional products. Millions of people around the world have learned to play music using John's easy-to-follow, accelerated programs.

John is a virtuoso musician who has worked with some of the industry's most legendary entertainers. He has the ability to break down, teach and communicate music in a manner that motivates and inspires others to achieve their dreams of playing an instrument.

As a musician and songwriter, John blends together a unique style of rock, metal, funk and blues in a collage of melodic compositions. Throughout his career, John has recorded and performed with renowned musicians including Doug Wimbish (Joe Satriani, Living Colour, The Rolling Stones, Madonna, Annie Lennox), Grammy Winner Leo Nocentelli, Rock & Roll Hall of Fame inductees Bernie Worrell and Jerome "Big Foot" Brailey, Freekbass, Gary Hoey, Bobby Kimball, David Ellefson (founding member of seven time Grammy nominee Megadeth), Will Calhoun (B.B. King, Mick Jagger and Paul Simon), Gus G of Ozzy and many more.

To get more information about John McCarthy, his music and his instructional products visit RockHouseSchool.com.